Legendary Away Days

For our clients

Legendary Away Days

The Complete Guide to
Running Successful Team Events

KAREN COOLEY and KIRSTY McEWAN

GOWER

Published by
Gower Publishing Limited
Gower House
Croft Road
Aldershot
Hants GU11 3HR
England

Gower Publishing Company
Suite 420
101 Cherry Street
Burlington, VT 05401-4405 USA

The authors have asserted their right under the Copyright, Designs and Patents Act 1988 to be identified as the authors of this work.

British Library Cataloguing in Publication Data
  Cooley, Karen
  Legendary away days : the complete guide to running
  successful team events
  1. Employees – Training of 2. Teams in the workplace –
  Training of 3. Special events – Management
  I. Title II. McEwan, Kirsty
  658.3'124
  ISBN 0 566 08549 6

Library of Congress Cataloging-in-Publication Data
Cooley, Karen.
  Legendary away days : the complete guide to running successful team events / Karen Cooley and Kirsty McEwan.
    p. cm.
  ISBN 0-566-08549-6
  1. Industrial recreation. 2. Special events -- Planning. 3. Teams in the workplace. 4. Employee morale. I. McEwan, Kirsty. II. Title.

HD7395.R4C66 2003
394.2'068 -- dc21   2003048314

Typeset in Stone Serif by Bookcraft Ltd, Stroud, Gloucestershire
Printed and bound in Great Britain by MPG Books Ltd, Bodmin, Cornwall

Contents

List of figures

Contributors

Karen Cooley is a Training Consultant based in South East England. She is a Visiting Lecturer at the University of Westminster and a director of her own Kent-based business, Christopher Glen Consulting Limited.

Kirsty McEwan is a Learning Consultant and international Facilitator. She travels widely from her base in the North East of England whilst also supporting a number of one-to-one coaching relationships at any one time. Kirsty owns and runs her business, Kirsty McEwan Consultants.

Preface

Why we wrote this book

We wrote this book because:

- We're passionate about events
- We're passionate about them being run well
- We're passionate about people having a good experience whilst they're at Away Days
- We share a core belief in addressing real issues at events in a sincere and adult way

… so we thought, as we've got twenty-five years of experience and expertise between us and we design and run hundreds of events every year, let's create a guide for others that will transform a potentially tricky enterprise into a smooth operation.

This book is packed to the brim with ideas. It is indispensable when you are at the planning stage, designing the detail of your event and even when you're at the event itself. One of the things we especially want to offer you is a clear way of pre-empting any kinds of problems before they turn into crises.

With these nuggets of advice at hand, you will be able to concentrate all your energies into making your Away Days truly Legendary.

Acknowledgements

Thanks to Ian Cooley and Jordan Scheer for all their encouragement and for being so proud of us … and for being there with wine and warm feet after we've been burning the midnight oil.

Thanks also to our clients with whom we've built up wonderful relationships and who've helped us develop as we've helped them. We love working with you.

A special thanks to Simon Moss who brought us together to work on a team Away Day in the first place.

KC & KMcE
2004

Introduction

Finding your way around

This guide has been put together to help you find your way to the information you need as easily and quickly as possible. Although the book makes for a good read, we appreciate that you won't have time to digest it from cover to cover before starting work on your Away Day. We have therefore clearly signposted each section so you can go straight to the chapters that most interest you.

Our approach in structuring the guide was to think through every stage of the process logically from beginning to end and to include practical, realistic and no-nonsense information that you can use immediately.

You'll find advice for every stage of the process, from thinking about the conceptual design of your event through to carrying out the evaluation at the end of a job well done. We've even included warnings about the possible pitfalls, as well as advice on how to circumnavigate them with confidence. The 'Shark Alert!' sign will warn you of potential dangers. The guide divides into four parts:

Part One: Getting started

Part One covers first steps toward running an Away Day, beginning with the abstract design of the event and progressing to making detailed plans.

Part Two: Essential information

Part Two looks at issues which impact on every single Away Day. Even if you are experienced in running team events we recommend that you look at the critical advice offered in these chapters, which will help your event to be the best that it can be and may even prevent it from going sadly wrong. In this section you will find advice on:

- Cultural diversity and inclusion
- Health and Safety/Legal liability
- Setting, agreeing and using ground rules
- Communicating your Away Day
- Using facilitators and specialists
- Handling different event roles

- Troubleshooting
- Exercises to break the ice, to boost energy and to create legendary memories.

Although your skilful handling of cultural diversity and inclusion or Health and Safety may be taken for granted by participants, if you get it wrong the results could be devastating. Chapters 2 and 3 consider both the ethical and legal reasons for getting it right and show you how to go forward with care and sensitivity.

Do you have a concern about accurately setting people's expectations of the event and managing standards of behaviour and conduct on the Day? In Chapter 4 you will find proven tips for managing the event once it is up and running. In Chapter 6 we help you add the finishing touch of gloss to your event by using facilitators and specialists.

Part Three: The Legendary Away Days

In Part Three we address the 'main course' of the Away Day menu – a selection of Away Days to suit your particular purpose. Each Away Day has been given its own chapter which includes a definition of the Day, example objectives and a broad outline to suggest the shape of how each event might run in practice.

How do you know which Day to use? We show you the symptoms to look out for in each case so that you can choose which Day most closely fits the current needs of your team.

Part Four: After the event

Part Four shows you how to tie up loose ends after the event through evaluation.

In our Appendices you will find:

- A checklist to help you get started
- A choice of room layouts
- Various tools and strategies
- A selection of feedback forms – all you need do is choose the one that best suits you.

Whatever aspects of running team events you're looking for, you will find them in this book. Our intention is not to be prescriptive, but to offer our experiences as a guide to assist you in running superb team events.

Good luck with your Away Days – may they all be legendary!

ONE *Getting Started*

1 *Organising your Thoughts*

You've made the decision to hold a team event. Congratulations!

This exciting decision will involve a considerable expenditure of time, energy, effort, and expense on your part as well as for others. It therefore makes sense to be crystal clear about the boundaries and objectives for your event before committing valuable resources. The planning and groundwork that you put in at this early stage will not only earn significant dividends later on, but are also likely to prevent an enormous amount of wastage and embarrassment. After all, you would not hold a dinner party without inviting people, planning the menu, checking for dietary needs and preferences, would you? Imagine serving with pride plump rump steaks, only to hear your guests utter 'sorry … we're vegetarians!'; The result? Red faces all round, which could so easily have been avoided had you thought ahead and followed a number of simple rules about planning; in other words, had you invested the time to think about and define the parameters of your dinner party. The same rules apply to your team event.

We see a fundamental distinction between cracking the concept of your event (that is, appreciating and planning the conceptual design of the day) and planning the precise practicalities involved. The former is about establishing the general shape, outline and tone of your day and understanding why you have chosen to hold it at all, whilst the latter is about planning the fine detail of the event – what needs to happen and how you are going to make it work.

Cracking the concept can therefore be equated to pencilling in your ideas and plans for the day, which can be rewritten and finalised in ink just as you finalise the *precise practicalities* later on. We see it as a two-stage process, with defining the principles and concept of your event as Stage 1 and finalising the detailed logistics as Stage 2. Although in practice you are likely to spend significantly longer at Stage 2 than at Stage 1, do not be tempted to cut corners and 'skate over' Stage 1, as it is here that the seeds of your success will be sown.

The following checklist will help to focus your thoughts before you jump in with both feet. Think of it as a guide to help you harness your enthusiasm, collect your thoughts and successfully crack the concept of holding your Away Day:

Stage 1: Getting cracking

At this stage the areas you need to think about can be organised into four sections (see Figure 1.1):

1 Your reasons for running the event
2 The type of event you are thinking of running
3 Taking account of any constraints
4 Other considerations.

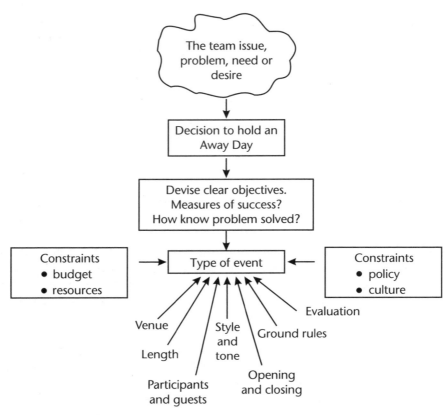

Figure 1.1 Stage 1: Essential first thoughts to organising your Away Day

YOUR REASONS FOR RUNNING THE EVENT

- Why are you running this event? Are you clear about your reasons for choosing to hold this particular event at this specific time?
- What is the intended style of the event? Is it intended to be an exuberant celebration, an information-sharing communication exercise or something more sober altogether?
- What are your required results or outputs? Are you clear about what you want to achieve from the event? After all, there is a world of difference between trying to encourage enthusiastic commitment to an eagerly anticipated and generally well-received new idea and helping people to cope with a potentially painful message, such as the need to adapt to a new situation following a number of redundancies. Similarly, you may be aiming to encourage a new team to bond and work together effectively, or working with a dysfunctional team to eradicate suspicion and mistrust amongst team members and go forward in a new, more positive atmosphere. Whatever your objectives for the team, if you don't define the purpose of your event before you begin, you have no measure of success against which to benchmark.
- What mindset and attitude do you want your participants to have when they arrive at the event? Start thinking about this now as it will impact on your choice of venue and the tone of your invitations later on.

THE TYPE OF EVENT YOU ARE THINKING OF RUNNING

- What type of event do you want to run? A workshop, seminar or conference? An indoor or outdoor event?
- What type of event is likely to work best with your planned audience (see Part Three for event types)? What have you done before? Did it work? Do you need to make adjustments to the format previously used, to suit the current circumstances? If so, what adjustments do you need to make? Remember that groups have their own specific characteristics. Try to avoid planning for an 'off the peg' solution.
- Start thinking about the type of materials that will be required, as some professionally-produced materials will have long lead times.

TAKING ACCOUNT OF ANY CONSTRAINTS

- What constraints have you got? What budget do you have?
- What resources are available to you, for example staff, facilities, materials?
- Have you thought about your venue in relation to these constraints? What will be the approximate size of the event? What can you afford? One of your biggest dilemmas about venue will be whether to hold it in-house or externally.

OTHER CONSIDERATIONS

We consider below some of the many issues demanding your attention in relation to your team event:

- Venue
- Length of event
- Participants and guests
- Style and tone
- Opening and closing
- Ground rules
- Evaluation.

Considering the venue

- What type of venue do you need to use for the event?
- How many attendees do you envisage?
- A large-scale auditorium, although imposing, could have the effect of either impressing or intimidating your audience?
- A small venue may not give you enough space, light or comfort. Select your venue type and location carefully: this is one of those times when size does matter!
- Much also depends on accurately matching the type of venue to your event as well as the culture of your organisation. This will often require considerable creativity: as an example, for organisations where outdoor events with plenty of fresh air and physical activity are welcomed, you might consider using a sports club, or even setting up some team games on a nearby beach if there is one.
- Will the event be run in-house or externally? Consider the following items:
  - Budgetary constraints.
  - Available feedback about previous venues used.

- Convenience of access for all participants.
- Whether you have access to experienced staff competent to design and run an in-house event?
- Do you have the time and competence to do it yourself? Remember that the consultation process can be labour-intensive so if you are thinking of taking on this task yourself, allow more time than you originally think will be needed for consultation and design.
- The 'message' you want the venue to send to your team about the importance of the issue.
- The choice of venue will send a message about how the team is valued.
- How much space are you likely to need? At this stage you just need to have a general feel for the number and size of rooms that you want. As a guide, the more space the better. Literally, room to think encourages creativity.
- Availability of refreshments. Do you want meals as well as beverages? Again, a general feel for your requirements is sufficient at this stage.
- Consider where you would like refreshments to be served. It is often best to serve lunch away from the main room so that participants get a change of scenery and are able to network. Alternatively do you want a working lunch? Stretching the legs and clearing the head provides an opportunity for people to regroup and chat to one another!
- Equipment: what do you need?
- Is there adequate on-site IT support?
- Will you need breakout or syndicate rooms?

Length of event

- What will be the length of the event? A half day, one day, two days or longer? Can you justify the length of the event if challenged? What benefits will the extra time provide? Think about any budgetary or resource constraints when planning the length of your event.
- Bear in mind your start and finish times for the event on each day. People will appreciate not having to travel to or from the event in rush hour if you can avoid it.
- The length of the event will influence whether you may need to plan evening entertainment. Think about whether you want to entertain people or will people be expected to amuse themselves? Keep in mind that bored participants quickly turn into unreceptive participants!

Your participants and guests

- Budgetary constraints may affect the number of participants and guests you can invite.
- Who should be invited to attend? Establish in principle the groups you would wish to have present at the event.
- Where will your participants be travelling from? You should consider venues in an area that is easily accessible. The Bahamas might be your first choice, but can your budget take the strain?
- Have travelling costs been taken into account?
- Will anyone require overnight accommodation? What type of accommodation will be offered and can you afford it?

Style and tone: getting the atmosphere right

- What mindset and attitude do you want your participants to have when they arrive at the event? Start thinking about this now as it will impact on your choice of venue and the tone of your invitations later on.

- What atmosphere do you want to achieve for your event? Having music playing as participants arrive for a Creativity Day might, for many, move them out of work mode and into a more creative frame of mind.
- Do you want the event to be participative and if so, how will you make that happen? Even where the event lends itself to a high level of participation, don't assume that people will naturally throw themselves into activities. Depending on how 'outgoing'/'shy'/'afraid of looking silly' they are, they may need varying degrees of coaxing before happily taking part. You may therefore need to implement some lower-level, non-threatening activities early in the day to build trust (between participants as well as with you) to gently ease them into the spirit. See Chapter 9 for a selection of icebreakers.
- What should be the overall tone of the event? Light-hearted? Weighty? Prescriptive? Consultative?

You will also need to think about how you want the event to run on the day: how to open and close proceedings, as well as how to establish guidelines for working together (see Chapter 4 for how to set ground rules).

Opening and closing your event

- Will there be a 'sponsor' to introduce and close out the event? If so, who? If you can persuade a key member of your senior management team to introduce the event with a few well-chosen and genuine words of welcome, and end the day with a similarly heart-felt vote of thanks to everyone for attending, you will add extra credibility to the Day. It shows that senior managers have a serious interest in seeing the event work well.
- Are you the most appropriate person to introduce and close the event? Sometimes it is most appropriate for department managers to take this role, depending on the reasons for the event. If the Away Day is exclusively for your own team, you may well be the best person for the job.

Running the event – ground rules

- If participants stick to agreed ground rules, would this help things run more smoothly? See Chapter 4 for how to set, agree and use ground rules and Part Three for some ground rules to suit different team events.

Evaluation (see Part Four)

- How will you measure how successful your event has been? It is not too early to think about your success criteria and your proposed methods of evaluation.

SHARK ALERT! POTENTIAL PITFALLS AT STAGE 1

- Do you feel that you really have the genuine support of senior managers for the event? Or are they simply paying 'lip service' to the idea? An audience will soon 'see straight through' insincere utterances from senior managers. If you are not convinced that they can add value to your event it is probably better to avoid having them there at all, assuming that you can stop them! If your senior managers insist on attending despite your misgivings, then you will have to adopt a strategy of 'damage limitation'. This may mean limiting their appearances as far as possible, possibly by inviting them to propose a short welcome at the start of the event, or by saying a few words at lunchtime. Try to go through the main points of their speech or script with them before the event to allow yourself the chance to influence their message.

- Who is the line manager of the team? It may be you, but if it isn't, check to see how the line manager sees their role at the event? How do *you* see their role? If the two views are different, how will they be reconciled? Above all, ensure that these differences are resolved before the day and are not played out in front of an audience.

Having taken account of any constraints and once you have a broad plan in mind, you can go on to Stage 2 and consider specific questions.

Stage 2: Planning the detail

From our own experience we now provide precise and practical detail in full as we guide you through the key areas to consider.

READY TO GET STARTED?

Are you confident that you have thought through the issues in Stage 1? Do you have a clear understanding of the purpose of your team event and the desired outcomes to be achieved? Once you have a good grasp of these points, as well as the scope, shape, style and tone of your event then you're well on your way and ready to start working on the finer detail of your Away Day – that is, on the precise practicalities.

We now show you how to plan your event in detail and lead you, step by step, through each part of an Away Day. Everything has been thought of. A well-planned event is far more likely to run smoothly and leave you with plenty of energy to lead or attend the event instead of worrying yourself silly and stressing those around you. What follows are the precise practicalities that you need to consider (see Figure 1.2).

SUPPORTING THE EVENT – FIRST THOUGHTS

- Will you need speakers? Will they be in-house or external? What value will they add to the proceedings?
- Who will facilitate the event? How many facilitators will you need?

EXTERNAL OR INTERNAL VENUE?

This will be one of the earliest questions that you will have considered. Once you have decided to hold an Away Day, one of your first and most important decisions is whether to choose an external venue or to run the event in-house. You may still have this decision to finalise. A variety of factors will influence your decision, not least of which will be the costs involved. However there are other factors at play in making your decision which, although they may not have an obvious and immediate financial impact, will have short-term implications for the success of your event and medium- to long-term impact on the success of your team.

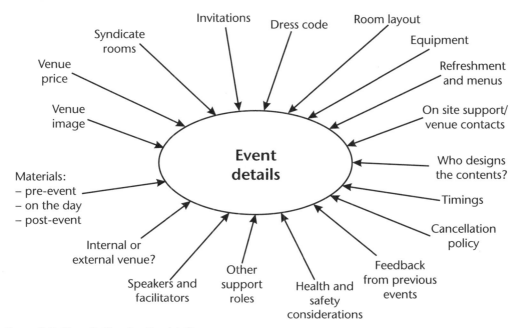

Figure 1.2 Stage 2: Planning the detail

What should you be thinking about?

Some guidelines to help you:

- What is the size of the event? This one factor alone may influence you to select an external venue. If, for example, you are planning a large-scale conference you may simply not have the necessary space or equipment available to render in-house facilitation possible.
- What is your budget for the event? Remember to take account of the fact that your finances will have to cover not only the direct cost of the venue but also the associated costs of the day – catering, administration, travel and possibly accommodation.
- Can you realistically resource this event in-house or will the level of support needed mean that you should be looking to go externally? There is a danger in relying on in-house administrators (who are possibly over-stretched already) to provide the quality of support that you need. In-house there is always the risk that participants will dive off to attend to work issues. This can disrupt your event timings and their train of thought.
- What is the purpose of the event? Whilst not impossible, it is undeniable that a Celebration Day is less likely to feel celebratory if it is held in an underground training room with no natural light and a plate of sandwiches for lunch! Each and every event sends out a message to colleagues – what message does it send if you hold an event in the dark and dingy basement underneath the luxurious offices of senior managers?
- What feedback do you have about previous venues used? If certain venues carry a good reputation, you must still visit them to establish your own views as well as your own rapport with the conference staff.
- Do you have access to experienced colleagues competent to design and run an in-house event? Are they creative enough to design a tailor-made solution or is there a danger that they will produce a tired re-tread of 'tried and tested' formats?

- Do you have colleagues available to help you stage the event?
- Availability of refreshments – do you need meals as well as beverages? Can your chosen venue meet your requirements? Do you want a buffet lunch or a hot 'sit down' meal? A buffet will allow people to mingle more easily; however a formal meal may be seen as more special and therefore appropriate as a 'thank you' to staff for a job well done.

What will your venue say about your event?

You will find external venues available at a wide range of prices from budget to luxury and while they will all do the job, they won't all send out the 'right' message to your attendees. Your choice of external venue will issue a powerful message to participants about the value placed by the organisation on not only the issues being discussed at the event, but also on the group itself. The investment you make in carefully matching your venue to your message may therefore reap you rich rewards in terms of respect and goodwill.

Reality check! Negotiate your venue price

Remember to negotiate your venue price – there may be savings to be made. There are also a couple of essential points to bear in mind before you begin. First, be realistic! It is easy to get carried away by the sight of an impressive venue or the promise of top quality service and over-reach your financial boundaries, but impressive venues and top quality service need to be paid for – do you really have the necessary funds available to settle the bill when it arrives?

Second, even if the initial price you are quoted falls within your budget, it is always worth checking with the supplier to establish whether there is any room for manoeuvre. Are you looking to hold your venue during a traditionally quiet time of year, when extra discounts may be available? Or can you negotiate on the basis of repeat business?

 ## SHARK ALERT! POTENTIAL PITFALLS IN CHOOSING AN EXTERNAL VENUE

Is your preferred venue in a sensible location for your event? Bear in mind that your participants may be making significant journeys to reach the venue. Do you need to provide transport for them, or will they be expected to make their own way to the venue and claim their expenses back from the organisation after the event? Remember that people will need to know about these issues early on if they are to make their own bookings.

Do you need syndicate rooms?

Whether using an in-house or external venue, how many syndicate rooms will you need to book? It is worth considering how your organisation runs its budget system. In many cases, the in-house rooms and facilities that you use will each have its own cost (down to the last cup of coffee) and all costs will be charged back to your budget.

Will additional charges be made for syndicate rooms? Although many external venues do make a charge for syndicate rooms, in many cases it is possible to acquire additional space for your event at a nominal rate – small rooms which may suitable as 'break out' rooms but which are too small to be saleable in their own right are a case in point. And you could use your requirement as a bargaining tool in the overall price.

Your decision on whether to book syndicate rooms (and how many) may depend on:

- the size of the main training area
- the type(s) of activities you plan to run

- whether you plan to serve lunch in another part of the venue, or have food brought into the main training area. If the group is likely to be based in the main training area throughout the day, a separate place for lunch will allow them a change of scenery.

SHARK ALERT! POTENTIAL PITFALLS IN ARRANGING SYNDICATE ROOMS

- Try to ensure that any syndicate rooms are situated close to the main conference area, otherwise the risk is that you will lose precious time on the day waiting for participants to return from their 'break out' session to rejoin the plenary group. Or even worse, you may have to waste time visiting the syndicate room to let them know when you need them back with the main group!
- Cost – try to plan for this. It is easy to say 'I'll have the extra syndicate room anyway – we may need it'. Will you *really* need it? Unless you can get it free you will have to budget for it.
- Be sure that 'free' syndicate rooms are 'fit for purpose'. Acquiring a syndicate room which is cramped or which has no natural light will be counter-productive – it may be 'free' in financial terms, however the risk to the goodwill of your participants is a price too high to pay.
- If there are no syndicate rooms available, think about using other public areas (for example, lounges) as mini 'break out' spaces for discussion groups. There are several potential pitfalls to bear in mind with this option:
  - Issues of confidentiality should not be discussed in open or public areas
  - Your group must not disturb others
  - Check that your group will not require any specialist equipment for this session which cannot be accommodated in the public area.

CHOOSING THE VENUE – OTHER IMPORTANT FACTORS TO CONSIDER

- Do you have any possible venues in mind at this stage? Have you used any of them previously? What was the feedback?
- Plan to visit the venues to check their suitability. This is crucial. What you read in marketing literature and what you get are not always the same! Has previous experience indicated that there might be any specific dietary and/or mobility requirements amongst your participants? Are you confident that the venue can cater adequately for them?
- Ask to view the event room(s), syndicate room(s), dining and refreshment areas – and bedrooms if accommodation is required. Make sure that you will be getting what you are paying for!
- Have you met your contact at the venue? Who will be looking after your group? Is there a Conference Manager assigned to your event? Who would deputise in their absence?
- Have you checked that there will be no building or construction work going on at the venue on the dates in question? Nothing is guaranteed to wreck concentrated thought processes faster than the noise of drilling or bulldozing while a group is trying to focus on essential questions or issues!
- Where would you like refreshments to be served? It is often best to serve lunch away from the main room so that participants get a change of scenery and are able to network – or do you want a working lunch? Stretching the legs and clearing the head provides an opportunity for people to recharge their batteries – and chat to one another!

AN OFFER THEY CAN'T REFUSE: MAKING YOUR INVITATIONS INVITING

With a variety of demands on people's time and with the number of options on offer, you need to pull out all the stops to make *your* invitation the most tempting. Here are some suggestions.

- Make it personal: mention the words *you* or *your* several times.
- Subtly flatter the person invited by referring to their needed expertise or skill.
- Offer the chance to meet others over delicious food.
- Make the invitation look professional: tailor it to your audience – will they respond to an informal, friendly style or does it need to be much more formal and status-conscious? See examples of two invitations on the following pages: one formal, one less so.
- Include with your invitation a list of who else has been invited and a programme for the event.
- Advertise your keynote speaker.
- Make sure that you send your invitations out far enough in advance that people have a realistic opportunity to attend. If you plan to send your invitations by e-mail, it is a good idea to set the 'receipt received' option so that the excuse 'it got lost in the post' can be discounted.

Formal invitation

Team leader/event leader's name

is/are pleased to invite *Professor Bigbrain* (plus all letters after their name) to the (name of event)

at (name of venue)

The purpose of the event is to (purpose) and we look forward to your expert input

Date of event

Start/finish times of event

RSVP to (name) by (date)   Keynote speaker: Dr Biggerbrain

Telephone:
Fax:
E-mail: Champagne reception to follow

Informal invitation (can be sent in paper or e-mail format)

Jane Bigbrain is pleased to invite you to your team Away Day on (date).

The venue for the event will be (name of venue). The Day will begin at (start time) and end at (finish time).

What is the overall purpose of the Day? (state)
What are the objectives? (state)

Please confirm your attendance by to (name) on (extension number) or fax/ email your confirmation to:

Fax:

E-mail: Invited speaker: Charles Biggerbrain, well- known for his knowledge on (specialism).

Dress code will be smart casual.   Thai buffet lunch will be served.

We hope that you will be able to attend: you can't afford to miss this event! We look forward to seeing you there.

Shark Alert! Potential pitfall

Aim to achieve a balance between giving people enough time to plan their attendance and giving them so much time that your invitation sits at the bottom of their in-tray pending their response. Chase up those who have not responded two weeks prior to the event. They may have questions about the invitation that they have not asked due to other pressures on their time.

A question of style

Making yours the 'must-have' invitation is largely about selecting the right style and wording to suit not only the occasion but also the needs of your intended audience. Think about what will really make it easy for them to accept. What has worked well with this audience in the past? What is the culture of your organisation? Is it a traditional establishment where people may expect a formal style, or a creative environment where managers are looking for innovative ideas and presentation?

Whatever your organisational style, a key success factor in your event will be inviting the right people along! Some points to consider are:

• Who are the key decision makers?
• Who are the key opinion formers?

and of course

• Who are the people who will actually do the work?

INVITATIONS – KEY POINTS

- Think about style. What will be most effective for you in terms of:
  - wording (formal, informal)
  - tone of wording (straightforward, jocular, irreverent)
  - colour (of paper and/or print)
  - font style
  - graphics (for example, corporate images or cartoons)
- Remember to tailor your invitations to suit the style(s) of your speakers as well as your participants. You are the PR agent for your speakers and you are responsible for representing them to your audience in a positive light.
- Give logistical information: participants need to know how to get there, what to bring, when to arrive, when the event will end, what facilities are available at the venue and, broadly, what the structure and timings of the event will be.
- Give clear guidelines on the dress code for the event.
- Prepare a programme outline with event objectives: this can be sent with invitations or at a later date.

Whichever approach you choose to take, a paragraph or two in the invitation for the event should help to focus people's minds on what is expected of them (and what they can expect of the event). Keep the details brief. Find an elegant balance between whetting their appetite for the event and giving them the essential information they need. Follow the old showbiz adage 'Leave 'em wanting more!'

INFORMATION ON WHAT TO WEAR

It is surprising how often the decision about what to wear to a team event can provoke confusion and upset among participants. The key question to ask yourself when deciding what dress code to suggest for your Away Day should always be: 'What recommendations should we make to help people feel most comfortable on the day given the environment and the types of activities planned?'

Although doubters may argue that a more formal approach will promote a business-like attitude to the work in hand, we always encourage a dress code consistent with the following factors:

- What is the event intended to achieve? If it is a conference, a more formal dress code (for example, business dress) may be necessary – if a teambuilding event, then 'casual' may be more appropriate unless corporate culture expressly precludes this.
- What type(s) of activities are planned? For events with physical (possibly outdoor) activities built in, casual wear (for example, jeans) may be recommended.

Defining 'smart casual'

Some venues and organisations request that guests and staff adhere to the 'smart casual' rule. This is what we understand it to mean:

- No jeans or trainers, no tee shirts, no sportswear.

Smart casual is a term that strikes terror into the hearts of some participants who may panic and go shopping for expensive designer casuals at the first opportunity. Whilst you may never completely abolish the element of competition implied by the term 'smart casual', you can help to eliminate the fear factor by specifying the dress code for the event in clear and simple terms. This may be as straightforward as, for example, 'Outdoor shoes are recommended for the afternoon session'.

Remember also that Equal Opportunities guidelines state that you cannot differentiate dress codes for men and women other than on grounds of Health and Safety.

GREAT EXPECTATIONS

Participants will want to know not only what are the overall aims and objectives for the event, but also brief guidelines about what is expected of them together with a programme outline setting out the 'running order' of the day. The programme outline can either be sent out

- with the event invitation, or
- at a later date.

SUPPORTING THE EVENT – THE SPECIFICS

Resourcing an Away Day can be as straightforward or complex as you choose to make it. The number of people needed to support your event will depend on:

- the number of participants
- the type(s) of activities you plan to include
- the size of the event
- the culture of your organisation – in some circumstances, involving members of the HR or training functions in resourcing the event may be desirable or even expected.

Ensure that you book your resources well ahead of time to ensure availability. At many external venues there may be a conference manager assigned to support your event. At other events you may choose to involve administrative support from within your own organisation. If you are using unusual exercises (see Chapter 9 for suggestions) you should book, borrow or buy equipment in good time.

CHECKING AND GREETING: THE ROLE OF THE RUNNER

Do you have somebody available who can take responsibility for working with the venue on the day(s) to rearrange timings as required, greet your speakers, find extra resources as and when required, check on absentees and generally iron out wrinkles?

ROOM LAYOUT

- See Appendix B for various suggested room arrangements (and suggestions for their suit-ability for different types of events).
- Tell the venue (or your Facilities department) which layout you require.

EQUIPMENT DETAILS

Your venue will be responsible for providing the equipment you need. Check that they have what you require. Your list could include the following:

- Overhead projector
- Screen to show acetates
- TV
- Video (possibly linked to TV) for playback
- Video camera equipment
- Extension leads
- PowerPoint
- Hazard tape (make sure that cables and leads will not be presenting any danger to your speakers, participants or facilitators)
- Microphones
- Podiums
- Flipcharts
- Pads and pens
- Computers
- Calculators.

Your list will be determined by the finalised programme content.

ON-SITE SUPPORT

Is there adequate on-site IT support? What is the likely response time for fixing an IT problem if something goes wrong on the day?

Ensure that you know who to contact in the event of an equipment failure. In even the best-prepared venues, the unexpected can happen.

EVENT TIMINGS

Be clear about your planned start and finish times and include this information in invitations. Agree the times for refreshments with the venue.

AGREEING THE MENU

Menus will need to be planned in advance with the venue to take account of special dietary requirements or allergies. Remember to ask for information about these (and mobility issues), and include clear references to them in your invitation.

IF THE WORST HAPPENS: CHECKING YOUR CANCELLATION POLICY

Perhaps the most frustrating budgetary waste is the unnecessary cost incurred through forgetting to cancel venues or services if they are no longer needed. What is the latest cancellation date, up until which you could cancel at no charge to your organisation? Check this, and then diary it a week ahead: this will cover you in the event of unexpected sickness, or large-scale cancellations close to the date of delivery, for example where line managers have prevented participants from attending.

A similar strategy is recommended when booking overnight accommodation for participants and speakers at your event. Overbook quantities, but ensure that you have a deadline for the final confirmation/cancellation date without penalty: and remember that if you are booking accommodation in any quantity, you *must* negotiate a better price to reduce your overall cost.

MATERIALS FOR THE EVENT

Start thinking about what materials you are going to need as early as possible to give you maximum flexibility if you need to change your plans, or if you get struck by a great idea nearer the time!

Pre-event materials
- Written articles as:
  - background reading
  - to focus thinking
  - to encourage discussion.
- Pre-event questionnaires to ascertain expectations and personal requirements.
- Reviewing reports: to 'position' the event by illustrating what has led to it taking place.

Materials on the day: handouts
- Do you need handouts, either as reference notes to support a speaker, or as explanatory back-up for a specific session?
- Can these be produced in-house? If not, negotiate a price with your printer: using quantity and repeat business could be useful levers for you.
- Whether your handouts are being produced in-house or externally, remember to allow enough time for the handouts to be prepared, proof-read and printed.

Materials on the day: visual aids
Will you and/or your speakers require visual aids, for example acetates or PowerPoint presentation? If so, do you need to format them for consistency with organisational 'house style'? Factor in time to:

- discuss with speakers the format they will require and let them know as soon as possible if you cannot provide this
- obtain visual aids from speakers and prepare in appropriate style
- either save visual aids in a format ready for use on the day, or forward them to Facilities colleagues who will be looking after your equipment at the event.

Materials on the day: exercises
At many Away Days, exercises and activities are an effective way of initiating and reinforcing new ways of thinking. These activities can range from relatively straightforward to resource (for example, flipcharts with pads and pens) to much more complex exercises which require a

shopping expedition! Whatever type of activities you plan to include, you will need to purchase or order materials in plenty of time.

INSURING YOUR EVENT

Insuring your event is about covering people and property against mishaps ranging from minor injury and damage to theft and disaster. In this section we cover the areas of insurance that you need to be aware of.

Employers Liability

This is a statutory liability which an employer is obligated to carry to protect themselves and their employees in the course of their work activities. Attending an Away Day is a work activity and is therefore covered.

Public Liability

Public liability is the legal obligation to pay damages arising from bodily injury, illness or disease contracted by any other person (other than employees), or loss of or damage to their property caused by the insured. Although cover is not currently a requirement of the Health and Safety Executive, it is important that external providers are covered in case they accidentally cause accident or injury to property or staff whilst working at your event.

Professional Indemnity

External helpers and advisers at your event, such as speakers or facilitators will often have Professional Indemnity cover on their own behalf. This covers them against any errors or omissions that they may make, including erroneous advice supplied to the client. As a client if you are engaging external speakers or facilitators you may wish to insist that they have appropriate insurance and even to see documentary evidence of this such as a policy document.

Medical Insurance

We would advise you to check your organisation's medical and travel insurance if you are taking employees away from their usual workplace. You may wish to purchase additional cover especially if you are going to another country (see Chapter 3 on Health and Safety). Doctors may expect payment for attending patients not registered with their practice, although this cost may be met through your organisation's insurance, or through an individual's travel insurance.

Refer also to Chapter 3 for information and advice relating to outdoor Away Days.

MUSIC LICENCES

If you are planning to use music or other soundtracks in your event (even simply as background noise to set the tone) there are two licences you will need:

- the Performing Right Society licence, and a licence from Phonographic Performance Limited.

Hotels and conference centres should have both licences, but you need to check that they do – if you are using a less common venue, you may need to apply for the licences yourself.

The Performing Right Society

The Performing Right Society works for composers and publishers who own the copyright on music. The PRS licence covers the premises where the music will be played and is usually reviewed annually. Holding a PRS licence will allow music to be played in public.

Premises at which music is to be played, whether it be at a training event or a social occasion, need to hold a music licence. According to the PRS, the responsibility for ensuring that the appropriate PRS licence is held rests with the premises. If, for example, a training provider goes into external premises and plays a piece of music and it is then discovered that the premises do not hold the correct licence permitting them to do so, there will be no responsibility on the part of the training provider.

It is up to the premises to decide whether they wish to exert a levy on the external visitor (for example, the training provider) for the right to play the music or use the hall for that purpose. There is currently no obligation on the premises to do this – it is solely at their own discretion.

There are currently 44 different tariffs in existence, each of which relates to a different type of organisation or a different type of premises.

For more information on the tariffs and the applicable regulations, contact:

The Performing Right Society
29–33 Berners Street
London, W1P 4AA
Tel: 0207 580 5544
www.prs.co.uk

Phonographic Performance Limited

As a general rule, when a sound recording is broadcast or publicly performed in the UK, a licence will be necessary. A licence will usually grant the holder the right to publicly perform or broadcast any of the songs in PPL's repertoire, and owners of sound recording rights can expect payment of royalties.

The PPL licence is also usually held by the occupier of the premises where the event is taking place. The licence covers the sound recordings themselves and is for the benefit of record companies, recording artists and musicians as the PPL works on behalf of record companies to collect royalties on behalf of artists. While PPL does not have the authority in most cases to grant licences for the copying of sound recordings it does regulate the public performance and broadcast of sound recordings, for example by radio stations. It is concerned not with the rights connected with the actual composition but with the recording of the composition.

Further details are available from:

Phonographic Performance Limited
1 Upper St James Street
London, W1R 3HG
Tel: 0207 534 1000
www.ppl.uk.com

COPYRIGHT

Copyright law exists to respect and protect the rights of the originator of (amongst others) an artistic, musical or literary piece of work. Copyright can cover films, plays, sound recordings and written published materials.

The period during which copyright applies varies. For literary, musical, dramatic or artistic works the period is 70 years from the end of the calendar year in which the last remaining author of the work dies (or the work is made available to the public, by authorised performance, broadcast, exhibition and so on) For sound recordings the period is 50 years (with the same provisions as above), for films 70 years and for the typographical arrangement 25 years from the end of the calendar year in which the material was first published. Although if these time periods have elapsed you will not need to seek permission to use the material, you may wish to acknowledge your source out of respect.

If you are intending to exhibit, publicly broadcast or copy the work of another person, the Copyright Designs and Patents Act 1988 gives that person the right to be identified as the originator of that work and to direct whether and how their work is used. This means that you will need to request permission from the originator of the work (or the owner of the copyright) if you intend to use it at your event. This can include film clips, music or readings. Neglecting to request permission is an infringement of copyright law and you should take care to ensure compliance.

For further information about this complex issue go to www.intellectual-property.gov.uk

Photocopying and use of copies

If you intend to copy material, apply to the Copyright Licensing Agency in the UK (details below).

The only other circumstance where it is permissible to photocopy material is where a publisher has indicated that all or part of a publication may be photocopied, for example where questionnaires or templates in a book may be copied and distributed for use at work.

For further information on photocopying contact:

> The Copyright Licensing Agency Limited
> 90 Tottenham Court Road
> London, W1T 4LP
> Tel: 0207 631 5555

AFTER THE EVENT: EVALUATING PARTICIPANT FEEDBACK

Effective participant feedback is key to checking whether your event has met its objectives. 'After the event' follow-up is dealt with in detail in Part Four, and you will also find a selection of pro-forma questionnaires in Appendices K–N.

Creating a legendary Away Day

You've chosen the most suitable available venue at the best price you can get. You know who's coming along, and why. Now is the time to design the content of your Day to make it a legendary experience for everyone.

2 *Cultural Diversity and Inclusion*

There are likely to be people from a wide variety of backgrounds attending your events over time. The question to ask yourself is how to make everyone feel and be included. Let's look at what that means for you as you plan and run your team event.

How do I avoid the risks?

You need to pay attention to the following:

- Everybody is different. Stay aware!
- Avoid offence – beware of humour that may offend any participant. Ensure that speakers and visitors to the event stay not only within the boundaries of the law but also within the remit of your organisation's Equal Opportunities policies.
- Avoid selecting words or phrases that could cause offence, for example suggesting that Scottish people are mean.
- Names: find out how to say each participants name in a way they like to be addressed. Correct other participants.
- Value difference: appreciate people's different experiences and acknowledge their viewpoints
- Ensure that everyone feels included. Remember to:
  - Design activities that everyone can participate in.
  - Involve everyone in all discussions and exercises, including feedback.
  - Avoid appearing to have favourites or focusing all your attention on one individual or group.
- Show fairness and objectivity in your decisions and processes.
- Ensure that your decisions are justifiable within the contexts of good practice and the law.

What do you need to think about?

We hear the above terms used frequently, but why do you need to be aware of them when organising, running and evaluating your events?

We think of cultural diversity and inclusion as covering:

- race
- gender
- religion
- age

- sexual orientation
- gender reassignment
- disability.

Shark Alert! Potential pitfalls

- Unknowingly discriminating because you think that you are acting in the person's best interest is no defence, for example not inviting Muslim colleagues to drinks after a Celebration Day because you are aware that they don't drink alcohol. The result might be that they feel excluded and upset: they might have been perfectly happy to attend and stick to soft drinks. You have removed their choice.
- Don't assume that because you are in a majority group everyone shares the same cultural values as you, for example that:
  - Everyone is married or wants to be married.
  - Everyone has or wants children.
  - Everyone can read and write.
  - Men can't talk about their emotions.
  - Women can't think logically.
  - Everyone is from a traditional nuclear family.
  - Everyone who classifies themselves as black has a dark skin: they may have their own racial definition.
  - You can tell a person's sexuality from their mannerisms and appearance.

Remember

- Check your own assumptions before you even get to the event.
- People in holes should stop digging. If you think you've made a gaffe, apologise: for example: 'I'm sorry, I've just assumed that everybody here drinks alcohol'
- Watch out for participants discriminating against others, for example encouraging others to break their religious rules such as eating prohibited foods. As a facilitator you have a responsibility to intervene and readjust the situation if you see that a team member has become vulnerable.

How do I handle emotional outbursts?

As facilitator or team leader, part of your role is to ensure that everyone feels comfortable with the way they are treated during the Away Day. Stay alert to the possibility that in certain circumstances, for example on a Challenge of Change Day (even where people have requested change) the reality may be that they are finding it difficult to cope with and may use emotive language and behaviour that causes offence. Although people may need an opportunity to express how they are feeling, if they are angry or frustrated this may be communicated through words and language that you believe are unacceptable. Whilst we encourage the expression of emotion because it avoids build up of resentment and sometimes gives useful clues to what is important to people, there will be limits to what you will accept. Whilst this requires careful management, missing the hidden messages being conveyed would be a lost opportunity to appreciate how people are feeling.

Try to maintain a balance between ensuring that you maintain control over such events and taking care not to stifle the flow of the event by 'policing' it overzealously. Our recommendation for facilitators is to take a firm approach but use a light touch. When managing emotional outbursts or a personal attack by one or more participants on another participant, always address the behaviour that you see happening in front of you rather than second-guessing the motives behind the outburst. Keep the volume of your own voice confident, using a neutral tone, and point out to the whole group the ground rules that have been agreed for the event. Your body language should be assertive throughout; neither threatening nor timid and hesitant. If the behaviour continues the next step is to speak discreetly with the instigator on a one-to-one basis in private and although as a last resort you can request that one or more participants leave the event, bear in mind that you are running a *team* event and that ideally you want to keep the group together.

Disability

Be aware of the way that people classify themselves. Ensure that you avoid jumping to conclusions about their capability and what they want and need. Ask people if they need help rather than just assuming that they need to be guided around an event.

Demonstrating sensitivity means that your offer of help is more likely to be well received, although don't be offended if it is refused.

Choose a venue with maximum access and facilities. Pre-event questionnaires should identify at an early stage any specific participant requirements (see Appendix D). You should ensure that you have made provision for these needs to be addressed at the venue.

On the Day, don't draw inappropriate attention to those who need assistance. Respect their dignity.

The event environment may need to be adapted to ensure that everyone can take part. You may need to take extra resources such as detailed handouts or material printed in large font.

Language

Language that is insensitive may upset team members. Condescension may irritate, as would pity.

We would highly recommend that if you are running a conference and have participants with hearing impairment, you provide signers approved by the British Sign Language Association.

As a facilitator you need to take care with not only your own language but also other people's to ensure that it is not offensive. This means constructively challenging those who make insensitive or offensive remarks and use of humour. Instances of sexist or racist language should be similarly challenged.

How do people classify themselves?

It is for individuals to determine for themselves how they like to be classified: it is not for others to do it for them. Never give people nicknames at an event or call them by terms of endearment.

Normality is in the eye of the beholder. One person's 'normal' may be another person's 'extreme'. We advise that the word 'normal' is avoided.

There are often groups who use what outsiders would regard as highly inappropriate terminology and humour in order to cope with the stresses of their work. You need to take this into consideration as a facilitator but not be drawn into following suit.

People use emotive terminology to express passions or dislikes and sometimes the expressions chosen can cause offence. The user may be oblivious to the impact of their words. Check your own terminology and discreetly challenge those who fall into this trap, for example 'When I did such-and-such, people around me must have thought I was having a breakdown.' Imagine the impact on participants who may have had mental health problems.

What is harassment?

The verb 'to harass' is defined in the *Collins English Dictionary* as 'to trouble, torment, or confuse by continual persistent attacks, questions, etc'. Harassment is often discussed in the context of sexual or racial discrimination. In this section we consider what it means to you as an event co-ordinator or facilitator if harassment takes place.

RACIAL HARASSMENT

The Commission for Racial Equality has defined racial harassment as 'an unwelcome or hostile act or series of acts carried out on racial grounds'.

SEXUAL HARASSMENT

We have drawn together, from a variety of sources, a definition of what constitutes sexual harassment and, importantly, what it entails and the signs to look out for so that you can deal with it.

Sexual harassment may be uninvited behaviour which is repeated despite the recipient making clear that it is unwelcome. The behaviour may leave the recipient feeling belittled, embarrassed, fearful, anxious, nervous and with their self-esteem damaged.

The behaviour may take the form of:

- Comment: light comment and jokes, or implicit and explicit threats
- Physical contact
- Circulation or display of inappropriate materials.

Guidelines for dealing with problem behaviours

If any of the behaviours outlined above take place at your Away Day, the following guidelines under racism and sexism may be helpful.

RACISM

Whilst there is now increased awareness around avoiding racism, there is still ignorance and insensitivity. The facilitator has a duty to challenge it and respect difference. Here are some points to help you:

- Racial or ethnic humour: avoid it as it can easily cause offence.
- Views and opinions that are expressed as comments made to an individual or made casually to the group may inadvertently offend or be calculated to do so. Avoid these unless they are expressed through self-classification, for example when a participant states expressly that they are a member of a particular group and have classified themselves rather than someone else doing it for them.
- Presentation or circulation of inappropriate material. As facilitator you must insist on its immediate withdrawal.
- Tokenism at events: don't expect one or two people to represent and speak on behalf of their race, ethnic group, gender, religion or specific group. Don't ask them to – it's not fair.
- Victimisation and bullying: when a team member is being targeted, either verbally or physically by one or more colleagues who regard themselves as more powerful than the victim. You are duty-bound as the facilitator to manage this. First, prevent it happening in your presence at the event. Ask the bullies to stop, and if they continue then expel them from the event. Second, refer the incident to the victim's manager (after the event).

Religion

Discriminatory behaviour may also be targeted at those with religious beliefs and lifestyles. Be really sensitive to the team you are serving by considering the following points when running your event:

- Remember not to hold your event on the dates of participants' religious festivals.
- Take into consideration special dietary needs.
- Allow observance of times for prayer and practices.
- Avoid using terms that may be considered blasphemous.
- Observe religious and cultural customs such as greetings, appearance and dress code.

SEXISM

Sexism is the unfair and unequal treatment of a person because of their gender. Here are guidelines to help you avoid it:

- Sexist humour: avoid it as it can easily cause offence.
- Views and opinions that are expressed as comments made to an individual or made casually to the group may inadvertently offend or be calculated to do so. They have the effect of reinforcing unequal gender difference.
- Presentation or circulation of inappropriate material. As facilitator you must insist on its immediate withdrawal.
- Tokenism at events: don't expect one or two men or women to represent and speak on behalf of their gender. It is impossible for one person to be a 'typical' man or woman: there's no such thing.

- Victimisation and bullying: when a man or a woman is being targeted, either verbally or physically by colleagues who regard themselves as more powerful than the victim. You are duty-bound as the facilitator to manage this. First, prevent it happening in your presence at the event. Ask the bullies to stop, and if they contiue then expel them from the event. Second, refer the incident to the victim's manager (after the event).

Sexuality

Discriminatory behaviour may also be targeted at a person because of their sexual orientation. Sexuality can be an emotive issue and you may have your own personal views on this, however in order to be fair and neutral, consider the following:

- Remember not to impose your own sense of normality on the group.
- Avoid verbal stereotyping or performing stereotypical actions.
- Acknowledge the validity of other people's lifestyles and have respect for them.

The Law

If you would like to know more about discriminatory law and codes of practice, you will find information on the following websites:

Equal Opportunities Commission www.eoc.org.uk
Commission for Racial Equality www.cre.gov.uk
The Disability Rights Commission www.drc.gb/drc/default.asp

3 *Health and Safety at Away Days*

Health and Safety is about protecting people by reducing risks to their well-being. The following questions and techniques guide you through the 'must-dos' of Health and Safety in planning and running your event.

Is an Away Day part of work and so subject to Health and Safety at Work legislation?

Yes. There is a dual responsibility in operation. Participants have a responsibility for looking after their own Heath and Safety and that of others, whilst employers must make workplaces safe and minimise risk to health.

All venues sell their spaces and facilities (including bedrooms) and are therefore subject to stringent Health and Safety legislation. They too are liable for any breach of the law.

We recommend that before running an event you carry out a Risk Assessment not only on your venue but also on the content of the event itself. Questions to ask yourself when carrying out a Risk Assessment on your programme should include:

- Is the programme content appropriate to the mental and physical state of participants?
- Do the participants have the ability (and just as importantly, the will) to take part in the proposed event? Have all activities been designed so that everyone can participate?

Assessing risk

Risk Assessment is defined by the Health and Safety Executive as 'a careful examination of what, in your work, could cause harm to people so that you can weigh up whether you have taken enough precautions or should do more to prevent harm'.

This examination should help you to decide whether a risk of harm is significant or small and this may depend on the type of venue being used.

If your organisation has a safety representative they can carry out the risk assessment for you however if you work for a small organisation without a designated safety officer you can carry out the risk assessment yourself, provided you understand what is involved. Check with the Health and Safety Executive who will advise you on up-to-date legislation in the UK and will provide a guide to carrying out Risk Assessment. Remember that you are responsible for ensuring that the risk assessment is effectively carried out.

What if my event is taking place outside the UK?

Your responsibility to your participants remains the same, although venues abroad may be subject to local legislation. Check this out in plenty of time before the event by contacting the relevant Health and Safety organisation in the country where the event is to be held. As a first point of contact for events being held in Europe try the European Agency for Safety and Health at Work which comprises representatives from governments and workers from its member states.

As a facilitator or team leader, what do I need to do?

There are a number of steps that you must take when organising and running an Away Day.

BEFORE THE EVENT – THE PLANNING STAGES

You must *always* make an assessment of safety for all those attending the event (including speakers, visitors and helpers), whether you are holding it at a hotel, a conference centre, or in a field! Your assessment must cover:

- the venue
- the equipment
- the activities (both indoor and outside)
- the providers: can they demonstrate compliance with the law?
- procedures, for example fire alarms, emergency evacuation, reporting of accidents
- materials

In its leaflet *Five Steps to Risk Assessment*, the Health and Safety Executive offers advice on the following stages of assessing potential hazards in the workplace:

1 Look for the hazards
2 Decide who might be harmed and how
3 Evaluate the risks and decide whether the existing precautions are adequate or whether more should be done
4 Record your findings
5 Review your assessment and revise it if necessary.

When designing your event, are you intending to hold an activity that could put people at risk, for example fire walking, parachute jumps or white water rafting? If so, you must check that the provider has the necessary registration certificates showing compliance with legal responsibility. Check whether you need separate insurance and don't assume that it is already in place *Don't ever force or pressurise someone into taking part in an activity if they don't want to.*

USING EXTERNAL OUTDOOR TRAINING PROVIDERS

If you are considering using external outdoor training specialists to run all or part of your Away Day, you should check whether they are licensed with the AALA (Adventure Activities Licensing Authority) as a licensed provider. Also ask whether they have been inspected by the Licensing Authority and whether they have carried out a self-assessment on their own safety procedures – and if so, when. Unregistered organisations may well run excellent and safe events, however you will need to satisfy yourself fully that they meet your Health and Safety requirements.

Make sure that you check the safety record of the provider and get copies of their written risk assessments for all your planned activities. This will also assist you in assessing the suitability of specific activities for your particular team. Also ask questions about the equipment that will be used. Is it checked regularly and maintenance carried out on an ongoing basis? What systems and procedures are in place in case an accident occurs? Who is responsible for safety within the organisation? And what type and level of training (both previous and ongoing) do the organisation's trainers receive? There may be additional checks to make – you can find out from the AALA. Remember to ensure that all participants have completed and returned a medical assessment form and that appropriate medical support will be available if required.

ON THE DAY: ASSESSING THE VENUE

If you are holding your Away Day at an external venue such as a hotel or conference centre, as we said earlier, you must make an assessment on safety. This will include checking the following:

- Room layout. All emergency exits must be clear. If any access or exits are blocked, get the venue facilities team to clear these before people arrive. If your venue doesn't want to do it, you must insist.
- Are there hazards in the room that could hurt anyone, for example electrical wires or cable that could trip people up? Get them taped down.
- Is there too much furniture blocking people's movement? Get it taken away by venue staff. Don't ask participants to move heavy furniture as they may injure themselves.
- Check for sharp edges; broken furniture or fittings that could cut.
- Worn or damaged carpets are common hazards. Get the venue to solve the problem.
- Check syndicate rooms and hospitality areas in the same way: if you notice any potential problems, tell the venue.

ON THE DAY: EMERGENCY PROCEDURES

- Inform participants in a very clear and simple way (using translators and signers if necessary). You must make sure that everyone knows what to do in the case of an emergency.
- Point out all emergency exits and where the assembly points are in the case of evacuation.
- Clarify the alarm sequences for systems testing and the 'real thing' so that people recognise the difference.
- Make clear the procedure to be followed in the event of 'the real thing'. As soon as you hear the alarm, don't stop to pick up your personal possessions, just leave quickly but calmly by the nearest emergency exit and assemble at the nominated point.

ON THE DAY: REPORTING ACCIDENTS AND ILLNESS

- The venue should keep an Accident Book by law. Report and note the details of any accidents (refer to Chapter 8 *Troubleshooting: the best laid plans* for dealing with injuries and accidents at team events). Be aware of RIDDOR (Reporting of Injuries, Diseases and Dangerous Occurences Regulations) legislation. All RIDDOR accidents should be reported to the appropriate Health and Safety Executive or local authority office. For a detailed list of questions to ask a provider before an event, look at the RIDDOR leaflet (see under *Further information* below for HSE website).
- Having looked after anyone who may have been ill with suspected food poisoning from the venue, you will need to report this to the hotel and ask them to deal with it. For further advice on this complex issue, contact the Health and Safety Executive or your local Health and Safety Adviser.

FOLLOW UP: AFTER THE DAY

You should send a report to your own Health and Safety Office outlining the circumstances and outcomes of any accidents or illnesses that may unfortunately have taken place during an event. This should be done as soon as possible.

Further information

More information, including the leaflet *Five Steps to Risk Assessment,* is available from www.hse.gov.uk

The Health and Safety Executive publishes a leaflet about RIDDOR, available on their website at www.hse.gov.uk

For further information on safety matters related to outdoor training, contact the Adventure Activities Licensing Authority on 01222 755715 or at www.aala.org

4 *Setting, Agreeing and Using Ground Rules*

Ground rules are a set of commonly agreed and understood guidelines which govern the process by which an Away Day will be run, as well as the standards of behaviour expected of all participants.

The development of ground rules helps teams to work cohesively. Ground rules even out the extremes. They allow the quiet ones to speak and the noisier ones to listen. Having ground rules gives licence to the facilitator and the group to refer to the structure as a way of managing disruption and disturbances without being autocratic.

Who leads the setting of ground rules?

The facilitator or the person who is acting as facilitator will lead the process. The whole group should have the chance to propose additions or modifications to ground rules as they are being introduced.

How will the ground rules be agreed?

The simplest method involves brainstorming the ground rules in syndicate groups or in plenary through open discussion. The facilitator can suggest certain ground rules if the group misses anything significant.

What commitment should be expected of each team member?

In agreeing the ground rules, each team member is making a commitment to themselves, their fellow participants and the facilitator to observe those ground rules throughout the Day. Each participant needs to consider; what am *I* prepared to do to help this process work?

This will include contracting to respect not only the process of the Day but also one another. You should encourage people to think about *how* they will act to demonstrate respect for colleagues and further the best interests of the whole team.

Once agreed, how will the ground rules be used?

Display the ground rules on a wall or flipchart so everyone can see them.

If a rule has been broken the group and the facilitator have an agreed right to refer to the ground rules in the hope that this will end the miscreant's behaviour.

 ## SHARK ALERT! POTENTIAL PITFALLS

- Encourage constructive ground rules rather than restrictive ones, for example instead of 'no over-intellectualising' put 'keep comments clear and easily understood'.
- There is a need to have ground rules as a tool for bringing the group back on track: however there may be a temptation to rush this part of the process. Allow enough time to develop them. This may take a little longer where the Away Day has been called to help a team operate more cohesively.
- Avoid getting obsessed with the laws and regulations. Ground rules exist to guide not to repress.
- Facilitate, don't lecture and reprimand.
- Occasionally you might sense unspoken resistance to proposed ground rules. If you think that adoption of a ground rule is especially crucial to get the team functioning properly (example: observing expected standards of behaviour) be prepared to suggest and reiterate the benefits of that ground rule without trying to impose it on the team.

Example ground rules: ones that worked well for us

- No hierarchy, even if in practice there is one in the room. We agree that there will be no 'pulling rank' by senior managers, as this will stifle creativity and freedom of expression.
- Mobile phones and pagers will be switched off. Where they need to remain on for unavoidable reasons they will be set to 'silent' or 'vibrate'.
- Everyone to participate. This means that everyone is encouraged to contribute their ideas, thoughts and comments as openly as possible, provided that their contribution supports the aims of the Away Day as well as their colleagues.
- Everyone's views will be of equal value.
- Focus on the main conversation and avoid side discussions.
- Constructive criticism of ideas is encouraged.
- Supportive behaviour involves encouraging and acknowledging contributions.
- Confidentiality: what is discussed in the room stays there.
- It's OK to have fun.
- Get to know each other better if this will assist group working (Note: this may be less relevant at a Conference Day).
- Work productively as a team.
- Challenge criticism of personalities (whether the individual is present or absent).

5 *Communicating your Away Day*

Communicating with your stakeholders

Your first decision will be to decide who your stakeholders are. Stakeholders will be anyone with a vested interest in what you are doing, ranging from people who are interested in the outcome to those who control your budget, or the public (if your team provides services and products to them). Stakeholders can include:

- Your team
- Senior managers
- Chief executive
- Your peers
- Managers in other departments
- Directors
- External agencies – they might not need to be at the event, but you might find it useful to let them know that it is happening
- The public
- Anyone who is impacted by the results.

There will be differences in how you will need to communicate with different groups of stake-holders. Some groups will simply need to know that your event is taking place out of courtesy while others will need to know much more detail, for example what you are trying to achieve and what decisions were made.

There are various ways of communicating with people:

- Newsletter (paper and email format)
- Intranet
- Exclusive report or as part of a periodic report (for example, monthly or quarterly)
- Presentation to the Board or employees
- Video.

You need to decide which is the best way to inform each group about the event.

Creating the right expectations for participants – making sure people are properly prepared

Deciding what you want or need to tell participants is the first step to creating accurate expectations. Things to think about include:

- Who will make the communication? When will they make it? How will they make it?
- Designing the right style of invitation.
- Sending invitations out in time (see Chapter 1 for ideas).
- What information needs to be included in the invitations?
- Warning people to prepare appropriately for the event, for example, to dress for possibly changeable weather if all or part of the event is to be held outdoors?
- Dress code.
- Clearly communicating the type of activities that will be included.
- Reassurance that the activities will be suitable for everyone.
- The objectives for the event.
- Expected level of participation at the event.

There may be other issues specific to your event. Ask yourself the question, 'What would I want to know?'

Post-event communication – communicating with people who weren't there

For a variety of reasons, team members may not have been able to attend your event. Groups in other teams may even feel resentful that their managers don't organise Away Days. Be aware of this and demonstrate tact when communicating your successful results.

- How will you communicate to team members? To other teams? To senior managers?
- When will you communicate? When the news is fresh is best.
- How often will you need to communicate? On a one-off or ongoing basis?
- What is the intention of your communication? To inform? To persuade? To educate?
- Will groups who were not there be invited next time? Will this need to be made clear?

How can we use communication to build on the success of our Away Day?

You could use the success of your event to promote the work of your team and enhance your career at the same time. Remember to highlight your activities and results to the right people using the right approach. Bear in mind that nobody likes a show-off!

6 Using Facilitators and Specialists

Do you want to add variation, authority and sparkle to your event? Perhaps you are thinking of buying in contributions from specialist speakers or professional facilitators? Where do you begin …? What is the process …? And how can you be sure that you're getting value for money? Whether you are looking to add authority by using a speaker with professional knowledge of a topic, or injecting a touch of vitality through the enthusiasm of a skilled facilitator, this chapter guides you through the stages of choosing and using external experts for your Away Day.

What do facilitators do?

Facilitate = 'to make easier' or 'to assist the progress of' (*Collins English Dictionary*)
Note: facilitators are sometimes known as *moderators* to recognise their skill in achieving a delicate balance between moderating differences in opinion and feelings whilst simultaneously moving the group forward.

The facilitator's role is to enable a group to achieve its objectives by literally 'making it easier' for them to do so. They are not there to instruct the group, or to impose their own ideas or opinions, but to help it steer a course to its intended destination. Whilst this can be a satisfying role, it is not always an easy one as sometimes there are obstacles needing to be cleared away before the group can even *see* the path, let alone negotiate it successfully. Obstacles may take the form of preconceptions, attitudes and behaviours that hinder decision-making and open, honest communication.

What skills and qualities do facilitators need?

Facilitation is a difficult job. We make no apology for the length of this list.

- Patience
- Tact
- Diplomacy
- Drive
- Tenacity
- Unlimited enthusiasm
- An unfailingly positive attitude
- Faith that the team will conduct itself positively and will not allow one volatile team member to blow it off course

- An understanding of the structure of the organisation and where the team fits into it
- Recognition that the group owns the problem and that it can select the process through which it reaches a solution
- Incisive questioning techniques
- Understanding that each group is unique and relating to it accordingly
- The ability to take a full and accurate brief from the client or in-house manager. Some questions to ask when taking the brief may be:
    - how do team members relate to one another?
    - what is the team's hierarchy?
    - what are the problems?
    - what does the team need to achieve? Where is it going?
    - what (in your view) would be the best way of getting there?
    - what processes have worked well with the team in the past?
- An understanding that at the beginning of the process, groups may need to share their concerns (these may be factual or emotional)
- Willingness to allow the group to discuss their feelings briefly about the outcomes achieved and decisions taken
- The ability to stay calm and not panic if things look about to go awry
- Intervention skills
- The ability to challenge entrenched views in a non-threatening style
- Empathic understanding
- Awareness of unfinished business so that it can be completed
- Knowledge of processes
- The ability to handle resistance and anger
- The ability to control damage caused by negative behaviour
- Knowledge of team dynamics
- A sense of timing and the ability to flex the programme to suit participants' needs
- The ability to 'read' the mood of the group and sense its needs.

Facilitators and specialists should:

- Help you design an event to suit your team's needs
- Add specific knowledge or expertise to your event which would otherwise be unavailable
- Be acknowledged experts in their field
- Be fluent communicators
- Be inclusive in their approach to the team
- Use a style that suits the organisation, for example use direct and succinct language if that matches the style of the client, and formality in tone and appearance to the more traditional and status-conscious
- Modify their approach to suit the message of the Day, a plastic smile for example is inappropriate when people are being told that they are losing their jobs
- Challenge thinking
- Complete the event on time
- Be diplomatic and polite, whatever the provocation
- Be able to fulfil a variety of roles: sometimes all at once.

Why should we enlist outside help?

Tempting though it is to take centre stage and 'do it all yourself', there will be times when to do so would be to court disaster. Don't be fooled into thinking that adding external specialists to your supporting cast reflects poorly on you and looks as if you can't cope. On the contrary, it is impossible to be an expert in every subject. Having the confidence, intuition and honesty to recognise when outside support is needed will give others more confidence in your decision-making ability. Why risk exposing glaring and critical gaps in your own knowledge when you can draft in specialist help that will strengthen and endorse your message?

Your own knowledge and expertise aside, a host of other pitfalls are lurking to trap the inexperienced facilitator.

SHARK ALERT! DOING IT ALL YOURSELF

- You may be too close to the issues and find it difficult to 'park' your own emotions and opinions while working with the group.
- You may currently not have the skills to be the facilitator.
- You may not have the time to spare.
- Whilst in purely financial terms you might think that you are saving money by running an event yourself, think also about the level of specialist knowledge needed. Are you discussing a technical issue where an acknowledged 'expert' might add credibility?

CLOSING RANKS: REASONS TO KEEP IT IN-HOUSE

Many of the reasons often cited for not using 'outsiders' simply don't hold water. Some of them are motivated by fear (of appearing unable to cope) and others by insularity. Here is a list that we often hear:

- External facilitators cost money and we can't afford them.
- They won't understand how we work.
- They won't understand the unique culture we work in.
- We have such strong personalities here: we are hard to handle.
- We can't expect someone from outside to understand the politics.
- We don't want to 'wash our dirty linen' in public.
- Won't it look bad if people think we can't manage our own event?

… AND POINTS TO THINK ABOUT WHEN MAKING YOUR DECISION

- What would be the cost of not achieving your aims or of mismanaging the event?
- Professional facilitators are practised at asking the right questions and quickly finding out what they need to know about your organisation, the topics being discussed and the dynamics of the group.
- External facilitators will incorporate the unique characteristics of your organisation and teams into the design of the Day. This will also inform how they relate to the participants, for example many teams in media companies find it easy to be open and honest with one another and so can be challenged to push ideas beyond their usual boundaries.

- External facilitators will be able to withstand the most determined provocation: it is what they do as a profession.
- Being one step removed from the politics will allow external facilitators to stay focused on the issues and not become distracted by personalities.
- Efficiently co-ordinating an event that incorporates impressive expert help will make you look *more* effective – not less!
- Have you considered how many external facilitators you might need? How much can you afford to pay? What will this buy you?

THE ADVANTAGES OF HAVING EXTERNAL FACILITATORS

Neutrality

Facilitators who are not directly employed can remain detached from the internal politics and interpersonal relationships that affect most organisations. If the Away Day stirs up impassioned emotions, a neutral third party will keep the team on track with a calm and dispassionate (though not uncaring) demeanour. With no vested interest in damaging the Day, picking favourites, or being emotionally involved, most facilitators only want the event to be successful.

Keeping the motor running ... helping to get the task completed

When teams stall or get stuck over issues, external facilitators will suggest several different ways of looking at the same problem to help the team get moving again. They will stand back and take an objective view of what is happening and why. If personal feelings are hindering progress, expert facilitators will help the group to face up to these: to understand and resolve them. They will also suggest what may have caused the blockage and enable the team to come up with their own ways of constructively removing it.

Managing time

Effective timekeeping is a vital part of the day. External facilitators are experienced at understanding when a group risks being distracted for too long by an interesting discussion that has little relevance to the main task. They are adept at refocusing the group on the central issue. It is essential to understand what can realistically be achieved in a session and to sense when the group needs to be moved along.

Managing dynamics

This is an area where the experience and professionalism of specialist facilitators comes into its own. Sensing when to pick up the pace with a quick energizer and when to ask the team to concentrate on a longer activity is a vital skill and although internal facilitators may plan for this, external specialists may have a broader skill-set to draw from. Their attitude will be 'if one activity doesn't work well, then something else will'. They will also be able to handle the interpersonal dynamics in the team.

We once saw two senior managers having a full-scale row in front of the whole group when the argument had nothing to do with the task at hand. Clearly there were some personal issues starting to threaten the event and we could not allow these to damage the good work being done by the teams. As facilitators we were required to challenge the two participants involved but this was best done in one-to-one discussions and certainly not in front of the teams.

Handling challenge

One of the key tasks of the facilitator is to supportively challenge participants to check their own thinking processes. Is their thinking sufficiently lateral? What has led them to their conclusions? Are there assumptions and stereotypes at work? How could they think about things differently?

Being skilled

This almost goes without saying: relevant knowledge, expertise and experience are 'must haves' for external facilitators.

HOW TO FIND GOOD EXTERNAL FACILITATORS

- By word of mouth
- By reputation
- Through professional organisations
- By meeting with them
- By watching them work.

… AND WHAT TO CHECK WHEN YOU FIND THEM

- When can you meet them?
- Can you identify what, precisely, they will add to your event?
- What type of industry experience do they have?
- Is their industry experience relevant to your team?
- How much relevant experience do they have?
- Have they taken an accurate brief? Can they help you with the design of your event?
- Will they let you watch them work? Although this may not be possible if other clients won't agree, hiring in external experts solely on the basis of recommendation without at least meeting them is a risky business and we advise against it.

SHARK ALERT! USING EXTERNAL FACILITATORS

- The group may be suspicious of having an 'outsider' invited into their midst. The perceived threat may lead them to close ranks and display a reluctance to freely air their ideas (and grievances) with the facilitator present. An expert facilitator will be able to work through this resistance.
- The external facilitator is removed from the day-to-day workings of the group. You will need to ensure that they are armed with sufficient knowledge of your organisation and the way the group works (both processes and group dynamics) to enable them to earn the respect of the group by 'speaking its language'.
- Check that your potential suppliers have significant experience of working in your industry in order to have credibility with the audience.

THE ROLE OF THE SPEAKER: CHOOSING A FLAVOUR

Above all, what speakers will add to your event is *flavour*. It is up to you to decide what flavour you want them to contribute. Do you need them to add a note of jollity and fun to the occasion, or to strike a note of sobriety? Speakers add an exciting twist to an event. Not only do they give your audience a different face to look at, but they can also lend a new perspective to topics that may already have been discussed in-house.

How and where will you slot your speaker(s) into your programme? Careful planning of the running order of your event will maximise impact. You might, for example, want to finish a morning session with a very upbeat, positive speaker to send participants into the lunchtime break on an optimistic, energetic note.

Engaging international speakers

The best way to do this, in our experience, is to ask international speakers to arrange their own travel to the venue, although you will need to arrange accommodation and, usually, transport back to an airport for their return flight.

CHECKING THEM OUT …

- Before you go too far in the contracting process, check whether you can see your prospective speakers in action. This will give you a unique opportunity to assess how they interact with an audience and to check that they will bring the desired level and type of expertise to your event. We have all witnessed the horrors of seeing speakers 'fall flat' because they seemed out of tune with the spirit in the room or because they bored the audience: or just as bad, they themselves seemed bored or unprepared. Doing your homework beforehand will help ensure that your speakers dazzle your listeners and this will reflect well on you.
- Can they recommend contact details for referees? Bear in mind that the referees given are almost guaranteed to be complementary about their performance: it would be a foolish speaker who would pass on negative contacts.
- What qualifies them as experts?
- Are they skilled?
- Are they credible?
- Can they impress with their presentation and knowledge?
- Be cautious about taking word of mouth recommendations. You cannot assume that what has worked well for others will succeed for you.

NEGOTIATING WITH SUPPLIERS

You will know what your budget figures are for the event and will no doubt be looking to cut your cloth to suit your means. Flexibility is an important factor: both yours and that of your supplier. They may be willing to charge less if there is potential for future business. Small operators may be more flexible on price than large corporations. Remember though, not to destroy any working relationship that you may have through your determination to achieve the best possible bargain. Here are some points to think about:

- Be clear about your budget before starting to negotiate.
- Be clear on what is included in the agreed price.
- Talk to the decision-maker.
- Check whether they have any previous relationship or connection with your organisation as this may affect their perspective on negotiation with you.
- Assess how much flexibility you have.
- Assess how much flexibility they may have.
- Be honest about the potential for future business.
- Remember that the supplier can say 'no': don't be shy of asking for the best possible deal.

BRIEFING SUPPLIERS

Responsibility for ensuring that the contractors are properly briefed is shared between the facilitator and yourself. Suppliers could be:

- Facilitators
- Speakers
- Venues
- Equipment providers
- Transport providers
- Caterers
- Exhibition specialists
- Entertainers
- Facilities, for example marquees, seating
- Printers and designers
- Public Relations specialists.

The key points are:

- Explain where they fit into the overall programme.
- Building relationships. Start on the right note by inviting them into your workplace (even if the event will be off-site) and discussing the event with them. Give them enough background to be useful, but in the case of facilitators don't break confidences about individuals.
- Give suppliers as specific a brief of your requirements as you can. Listen to their professional advice and incorporate it into the brief if you feel it is valid. Suppliers need to have a very clear idea of what is expected of them.
- Invite the supplier to ask any questions that will help them understand the event.
- Will there be an element of co-facilitation to your event? If there are other facilitators, are they clear on when they will be needed, and what they will be required to do?
- Discuss what level of support each supplier will need, both before the event and on the day.

EVALUATING SUCCESS: A FLICKER OR A FLAME?

You will want to know how well your suppliers have performed, for example did your invited speaker(s) set the place alight with enthusiasm, or did they turn out to be a damp squib. To get a full picture you must get feedback from participants (see Part Four). You should also request a brief report from facilitators and speaker(s).

The feedback that you receive on your Day will be valuable for:

- A record of what happened at the Day
- Any follow up that's required
- Participants' assessment of speakers – who was liked and who wasn't
- Design of your next event
- Following up on any feedback of a confidential nature with individuals.

Store feedback where it can easily be accessed for future use and above all, make sure that is used for future learning.

7 Handling Different Event Roles
Pilots, Shepherds, Playground Managers and Nannies

Differing dynamics: the need for different event roles

Are you facilitating the event yourself? If so, you need to think about the wide range of roles that you might need to play during the course of a single Away Day. Participants are able to alter the tone of an event within seconds through comment or action and you need to be constantly alert for changes in the group dynamic.

This chapter outlines the most common event roles that you may need to take and the skills needed to successfully fulfil them. The event roles are:

- Pilots
- Shepherds
- Playground managers
- Nannies.

PILOTS

Pilots help the team to navigate its way through any misty patches or periods of uncertainty during the Day. This may involve offering an initial version of what you see going on in the team and inviting the group to confirm, correct or develop this further. An example would be when the team is going round in circles in its attempt to reach consensus or make a decision.

Pilots have the advantage of being able to take an overall snapshot view of the team objectives as well as how the group is working together. They can use this view to help the team map out a clear direction to follow. From time to time the group may need to stay with an issue until they are sure that they are heading in the right direction and if necessary refocus.

When to pilot the team
- If you believe that the team is losing its way, check that everyone understands the issues and that they know what needs to be done to resolve them.
- When you feel that too many comments are being offered at once, clarify the main objectives.
- If there is a risk of the issues becoming distorted or misunderstood, stop the discussion and check that the whole group understands.

- If you see the team trying to take the arduous route to reaching an answer; the pilot could offer an alternative process, or at least ask the group to think of one.

SHARK ALERT! POTENTIAL PITFALLS FOR PILOTS

There are dangers inherent in offering an alternative process: the group may have made an emotional investment in their initial process and might resent any suggestion that there is a better way. Offer the group the challenge of finding a better way but don't veto their initial idea. Setting a time limit concentrates minds!

Key skills for pilots

- The ability to retain sight of the 'wider picture'.
- Analytical skills: is there a more timely way of achieving the group aims?
- Facilitation skills: the capacity to encourage alternative thinking without appearing patronising or adopting ownership of the issues.
- The ability to empathise with the group without becoming emotionally entangled with their opinions.
- The ability to listen and assimilate any hidden messages. What are people saying and what do they mean?
- Constructive challenging can be a helpful tool to clear away old thinking.
- Summarising to constantly keep everything in perspective

SHEPHERDS

From time to time the facilitator or event leader will need to lead a group gently but firmly toward an agreed course of action. The need to 'shepherd' sometimes occurs where the agenda is falling seriously behind time, either because the team are enjoying themselves so much that the clock is being ignored or they are so deep in discussion that they need reminding of their deadlines. At this point shepherds will need to summarise where the team has got to and check any need for additional discussion: if this is required, review (and perhaps revise) the Day's activities to accommodate this.

At other times, the group may appear in danger of discussing a point to destruction (the law of diminishing returns). Is the extra time spent talking resulting in a better quality decision? To avoid this happening, step in and direct the group to the key agreed objectives. Ask:

- 'How is the discussion contributing to the achievement of the objectives?'
- 'Is the group seeking a "must have" or a "nice to have" solution?'

If the group want to continue talking, let them know their options; something will be lost from the rest of the agenda. What do they want it to be?

When to shepherd the team

- If timings seem to be in danger of seriously falling behind.
- When the team seems to have identified the solution to a problem and are repeatedly debating the 'whys and wherefores' of the solution.
- Where the group has gone off at a tangent and is in need of being pulled back.

SHARK ALERT! POTENTIAL PITFALLS FOR SHEPHERDS

- There may be an assumption that you have all the answers. Use your gut instinct and then check with the group. Is what they're doing heading them in the right direction? Ask: 'Is this the best way we can do this right now?'
- Being *so* gentle that people don't pay attention.

Key skills for shepherds

- A gently persuasive approach; and a firmly persuasive approach if the first one doesn't work!
- A flexible attitude. People may raise relevant points when the facilitator or event leader tries to shepherd them along. Be prepared to listen to these, as the group may need to hear and evaluate them before moving on. Dismissing them not only risks losing an important perspective but also builds resentment.
- Be sensitive to any resistance shown by the group. They may feel that they are being rushed. Ensure that this is not the case by checking whether there are any outstanding comments before moving on.

PLAYGROUND MANAGERS

Playground managers need to employ a range of skills that might seem more suited to the schoolyard than a team event. Whilst group members might be aware on a rational level of the need to treat one another with a mature and adult approach, sometimes personality clashes surface with the result that the protagonists act like naughty children. Irrespective of whether the background to this is rooted in personal dislike or political baggage from work, you cannot allow this sideshow to derail the group.

When to be a playground manager

- If two or more participants are indulging in low-level childish, hostile behaviour toward one another, for example demonstrating negative body language when the other is speaking or verbally undermining them. Refer them to the ground rules or just ignore them if their behaviour is not undermining the group process. It is up to you to make a judgement.
- Where higher-level aggression is apparent, for example shouting the other person down. Do not try to handle this in the room. Speak with the protagonists outside.
- When two or more team members are sniping at each other on the sidelines rather than raising the issues openly. Keep them in separate groups as much as possible and tell them that you would appreciate it if they would stop doing it.

SHARK ALERT! POTENTIAL PITFALLS FOR PLAYGROUND MANAGERS

- Becoming embroiled in the dispute at the expense of group progress.
- Not treating everyone the same when managing childish behaviour.

Key skills for playground managers

- Neutrality: don't take sides in disputes.
- A resolute but supportive demeanour. Sometimes there will be a need to speak with the two protagonists on a confidential basis away from the main group. This should take place as soon as practicable once you have recognised the problem.

- Finely-tuned listening skills.
- Use a placating tone of voice that won't be interpreted as antagonistic or sarcastic.
- Tact.
- Diplomacy.
- Effective questioning techniques.
- Sensitivity to how the dispute might be affecting the rest of the team.
- Desire to find a way to work together that satisfies both parties – at least partially.

TAKING THE MEDICINE: THE NANNY

The 'nanny' role comes into play if the team has been through a difficult period and is feeling vulnerable as a result. Examples of this might be following a merger or acquisition, or a period of organisational restructuring. The 'nanny' will appreciate what the team has experienced but will not allow it to wallow in self-pity. Instead the focus will be on a no-nonsense and pragmatic look towards the future, with support provided for those who require it.

When to 'nanny' the team
- Following periods of trauma for the team, such as merger with another organisation.
- When redundancies have taken place, being aware that people might be going through a sense of loss.
- Where there are rumours of impending redundancies.
- Where significant change has been foisted onto the team without consultation.
- Where key results have been disappointing, leading to a period of uncertainty.
- Where the team has unsympathetic or 'difficult' leadership.
- Where the culture of the organisation has changed dramatically.

SHARK ALERT! POTENTIAL PITFALLS FOR NANNIES
- Appearing to side with the team against its leadership.
- Patronising the team.
- Sympathising instead of empathising.
- Doing things for the team instead of helping them to do it for themselves.

Key skills for nannies
- Communicating firmly.
- Compassion.
- Empathy.
- The ability to focus on the future without appearing to disrespect or diminish the past.
- Genuinely appreciating how people are feeling. Acknowledging that their feelings are valid for them.

CHAPTER

8 *Troubleshooting*
The Best Laid Plans

Whilst there may seem to be countless potential problems waiting to upset your best laid plans, knowing how to switch to Plan B at a moment's notice will give you confidence in handling any eventuality. In this chapter we explore a range of possibilities and provide tried and tested suggestions on how to safely manage what can go wrong with the Away Day environment and the human dynamics factor. Trouble usually appears in one or more of the following guises:

- People
- Materials
- Equipment
- Venue.

Let's start by looking at the most inspiring (and possibly the trickiest) of the four problem areas: people.

Handling humans: behaviour, actions, relationships

The one certainty when working with others is that at some point they will surprise you. Occasionally they will delight and enchant you; just as often, they will exasperate, infuriate and drive you round the bend! Once this is recognised and understood, you will be better prepared to handle the rewarding (and frustrating!) experience of working with others to design and deliver a team event. We list below the most common 'people' problems that you are likely to encounter on the Day.

 ### SHARK ALERT! 'PEOPLE' PROBLEMS

- People don't want to participate
- There is rebellion afoot
- Illness or injury strikes
- Scepticism is rampant
- Speakers are delayed
- Speakers don't arrive.

GUIDELINES FOR RESOLVING 'PEOPLE' PROBLEMS

- Tackle the problems. Ignoring them doesn't mean that they will go away.
- Don't make people look or feel foolish, either intentionally or unintentionally. For many, confidence is fragile; hard to develop and easily destroyed.

- Never join in with those who may be trying to undermine others. Instead refer back to your ground rules.
- Don't bully! Beware of appearing to push people into contributing unwillingly, as the group will recognise and resent this.
- Recognise that the reticence is unlikely to be personal and don't panic.
- Stay focused and in control.
- If people are not clear about the topic or the process of the Day, take time to clarify. Although it may initially cost you some time, you can only help the group move forward if they are confident that they are tackling the right issues and understand the process. If you don't do this you risk turning them off.
- Keep everyone involved: watch for people 'drifting' off.

What happens when the audience doesn't want to participate?

People may be reluctant to contribute for one or more of the following reasons:

- Shyness.
- Fear of looking silly.
- Lack of interest in the topic.
- The brief may have changed. Perhaps the leader of the group (who briefed you) got it wrong. Sometimes the general's view of an issue is not the same as that of their troops.
- Disappointment in the event; perhaps they would have done it differently.
- Lack of understanding of the topic and its importance.
- Lack of understanding of the process of the day.
- People may be fatigued due to lengthy journeys and early start times. Were your venue location and start times properly thought through?
- Personality clash with others in the group.
- Desire to damage group dynamic (feelings have to be running *really* high for this to happen).
- Arrogance or superiority complex on the part of one or more participants.
- Anger at the organisation and its imposed changes.

Switching to Plan B: how to combat non-participation

- Raise your own energy levels.
- Remain encouraging; stress that all contributions are welcome.
- Stay positive; don't be downhearted because Plan A didn't work.
- Don't take it personally if people don't want to participate. Sulking will *not* endear you to the group. Smile through the pain!
- If people are reluctant to take part for fear of looking silly, give them an opportunity to contribute anonymously. Invite questions to be written down on cards and put all the cards into a hat. You can then address all questions in turn.
- Challenge arrogance through skilled questioning. Remember that arrogance can mask insecurity; perhaps the person is feeling threatened (for example by change). Don't argue or let a battle of wills develop. Keep the whole group involved and focused and don't concentrate all your energy on trying to win over one person. Where the root cause of arrogance is a superiority complex, groups will frequently apply a subtle dynamic of their own, allowing the individual to express their views while making it clear that this will not derail the group process. Trust in the group that they will exert a positive influence and try to stay calm. If the individual doesn't respond, simply move on.

What if I am faced with mutiny?

This is the nightmare scenario and is thankfully rare. If it does seem that you are facing whole-sale rebellion from the group, for example, they have been forced into attending and are displaying intense resentment, you may need to stop the process completely and work with the group to identify precisely what the problem is. This takes courage. It can be unnerving for even the most experienced facilitator, however if you can stay calm and focused it may be your only option. Our advice is to:

- Keep calm, even if you don't feel it.
- Stay in control of yourself: your tone of voice and body language will send out powerful messages about how you feel.
- Give the group choices about the way forward. Be realistic and sensible about the choices you give. This will keep the group involved and will lessen the charge that they are being marginalised. Then ask them to make the decision as this gives them responsibility and the burden is not all yours.
- Allow the group some breathing space. Taking a few minutes to go away and make a decision about the direction of the day will allow emotions to cool.

What if the leader undermines the group? Controlling damage

If a leader has undermined the group at their Away Day, it may leave members of the group feeling hurt and de-motivated. How do you limit the damage that's been done? We suggest you take the team away from the leader by suggesting an exercise that involves group work (*without the leader's involvement – but do not state this explicitly!*) Meanwhile, talk to the leader, giving feed-back on what you've observed happening as a result of the leader's input and ask for, or suggest, a solution. If you find this difficult to do, concentrate on motivating the group rather than confronting the leader. Consider asking the group what would motivate them. Based on the suggestions, act as a bridge between the leader and the group by asking key questions such as:

(To the leader) 'Can you support that idea?'
'What would need to happen for you to support that idea?'
'Can the team moderate that idea so that you will support it?'

This means looking for what *is* possible in each party's suggestion, rather than what *isn't*.

WHAT IF SOMEONE FALLS ILL OR IS INJURED DURING THE EVENT?

This rarely happens at an event. If it does occur, the concern of the event organiser must be for the well-being of the participant, *not* with pointing the finger of blame (in the case of accidents). In the rare cases where the facilitator believes that the behaviour of one or more participants is endangering the safety of others, the facilitator should quietly but firmly ask the offending participant to leave the event.

In the case of accidents you will need to notify the venue and complete an accident report. Most venues will have a first aid room or a private area where people can rest if they are feeling unwell. Do the following:

- Find out who to contact for first aid
- Find out how to contact them

- Arrange for them to see the sick/injured participant as soon as possible
- Consult them on next steps – do you need an ambulance to attend?

As the person responsible for the event, don't allow a heroic participant to refuse the offer of first aid or medical help if you think it is necessary.

What do I do if the situation looks serious and no first aid assistance is available?

If you believe that hospitalisation is necessary, ask someone to call an ambulance immediately. Ensure that the participant's team is aware of what has happened. See Chapter 3 (page 32) for reporting of accidents.

WHAT TO DO WITH CYNICISM

If cynicism exists it will soon become apparent, in the form of sarcastic comments, sceptical 'asides' and a frosty atmosphere in the room. Causes vary from group to group, but could include one or more of the following:

- The topics to be discussed on the Day have been debated before, with no tangible outcome.
- The team have little faith that agreed outcomes will be implemented (they may for example have no confidence in the competence of those tasked with implementation or the commitment of key decision-makers).
- The group think that their time could be better spent discussing other issues.
- Unrealistic expectations were set last time.

How do I handle it?
- Clarify the background to the Day and briefly outline the reasons why the topic is being debated again. If challenged, be open about the fact that previous outcomes were disappointing; allow people to express their feelings, but don't blame individuals for the lack of results last time.
- Focus on the future. How much time has elapsed since the last time this was discussed? What has changed? Emphasise the need for a clear Action Plan to be owned by the whole group who will share responsibility for moving it along.
- Be receptive to what people are saying without being drawn into taking sides.
- Be encouraging and realistic about what can be achieved on the Day and what follow-up needs to happen afterwards.

WHAT IF SPEAKERS ARE DELAYED?

If a message is received that the speakers are delayed, there is a chance that they will miss their allocated slot. Be prepared to reshuffle the running order of your event to accommodate this, although it might involve some diplomatic discussion. Remember that the venue is there to support you. Other speakers and facilitators will usually help you out, if you approach them in a way that flatters them and expresses appreciation (there's no need to be too sickly).

WHAT IF SPEAKERS DON'T ARRIVE AT ALL?

If there has been no message from your speaker and no appearance and your attempts to contact them have been fruitless, by now you suspect that they aren't going to arrive at all. Switch to Plan B immediately. Your options include:

- *for in-house events:* it is time to draft in your 'substitute' speaker – yes, you should have one. Use your networking skills to cultivate a coterie of friendly managers who will help you in a crisis. When you introduce them, apologise on the original speaker's behalf and promise to explore rescheduling them at a later date. Stress the benefits of this rare opportunity to hear the new speaker before handing over to them.
- *for external events:* apologise on the speaker's behalf for their absence. Facilitate a replacement activity that you can deliver within the available time. Be sure that the replacement complements the rest of the programme otherwise it will do more harm than good. If you do not have a replacement activity and you are planning on moving to the next agenda item, ensure that you keep the venue up to speed – can they accommodate any changes to planned refreshment breaks?

Troubleshooting problems with materials

You might expect to be on safer ground with materials than with people; after all, paperwork doesn't have a mind of its own! Even so, think about the possible scenarios.

SHARK ALERT! 'MATERIALS RELATED' PROBLEMS

- The venue loses the materials you planned to give out to participants.
- Your visual aids (acetates, disks, demonstration items) have not arrived at the venue.

GUIDELINES FOR RESOLVING 'MATERIALS RELATED' PROBLEMS

- Prepare a set of master documents and take them with you in a plastic wallet or on disk.
- Have your documents sent to the venue in good time before the event. Two or three days should be sufficient.
- Check the day before that your documents have arrived at the venue.
- Try not to be 'rattled' by the loss of your visual aids. There is a way round every problem provided that you stay in control: of yourself!
- Stay civil to your contacts at the venue. Most will help if you are polite.

What if the venue can't find my materials?

If you have sent your materials to the venue, clearly marked and in good time, but the venue claims no knowledge of them, what do you do?

- First, check with your given contact at the venue (as opposed to Reception). Do you know who was the carrier responsible for transporting the documents? If you have time, have them contacted.

- If your documents can be traced, is there time for them to be delivered before the event starts, or do you need to switch to Plan B immediately? Having them couriered too late for the event is a waste of money.
- Source a flipchart, with flipchart pads and coloured pens. It is a good idea to carry your own set of coloured flipchart pens as those provided by venues cannot be relied on.

Plan B for your materials

There are two stages to Plan B:

1 Thinking ahead
2 Reacting on the day.

Thinking ahead   Take a master set of all your documentation and visual aids (hard copy and disk). In an emergency most venues will photocopy what you need.

Reacting on the day   If the venue can't supply copying support, delegate a trip to a local printers.

The quality might not be quite what you'd intended but don't get hung up about it at this stage; this *is* an emergency. Don't mention it to the audience. Only tell them that you've had an emergency if comment is passed.

Photocopy what you really need at the event (the *must haves* rather than the *nice to haves*). Otherwise tell the group that a set of reference documents will be sent to them shortly after the event.

The nightmare scenario – what if I've lost my own master set?

Flipchart the main points and use them as a springboard for discussion. Act with confidence and remember two things:

- This eventuality is unlikely to be fatal: although it may seem so at the time.
- People didn't know what you were going to say, so they won't know what they're missing.

Whilst materials lend valuable support, remember that *you* are the star turn. Keeping cool and concentrating on your delivery is ultimately more important than having the perfect props.

Troubleshooting problems with equipment

Equipment, like paperwork, sometimes appears to have a life of its own. These are some of the troubles we have encountered with equipment and how to deal with them.

SHARK ALERT! 'EQUIPMENT-RELATED' PROBLEMS

- Data and computer links aren't operational
- The OHP isn't working
- The TV or video breaks down
- The power goes off
- Audio systems (for example, microphones) become soundless.

GUIDELINES FOR HANDLING 'EQUIPMENT-RELATED' PROBLEMS

- Arrive early and test equipment before you start
- Notify the venue of problems as soon as possible and demand that they are rectified
- Take action and advise participants on a 'need to know' basis
- Try to keep your sense of humour
- Be tenacious
- Be flexible. Find another way to get your message across.

WHAT IF EQUIPMENT FAILS ON THE DAY?

We've experienced everything from overhead projectors held together with sticky tape to electrics that failed in a large lecture theatre filled with students. We survived and so can you. Here's how:

Data and computer links aren't operational

This is where hard copies will save you. Use your acetates. If a session involves internet dial-up then be prepared for it not to work: ensure that the dial-up is not the full purpose of the session and you have other objectives to cover.

The OHP isn't working

Test it before you start. It is usually the bulb. This is easy to replace and will only take the venue minutes to fix. If it still doesn't work get the venue to supply another OHP or resort to putting the main points up on flipcharts instead.

The TV/video has broken down

Check it before you start. Give this issue straight to the venue or the hiring company – expect them to either talk you through what to do or come and mend/replace it. Revise your running order accordingly and tell the participants. Plan B will include having a group activity available to fill time in case the worst happens. The guideline is to select

- an activity that does not require additional equipment
- an activity that complements the rest of the Day.

The power goes off

Getting the audience on your side so that they work *with* you is paramount. Use appropriate humour and ad-lib. If you are giving a speech, don't acknowledge the possibility that you are *not* going to finish. If you have a microphone, is it still working? If not then check that you can be heard. You may need to mingle with your audience to engage them (think chat show hosts). At least you can be heard, if not seen.

Promise to send out 'key points' of your speech to participants soon after the event.

Audio systems (for example, microphones) become soundless

See above, as it says it all. Just to remind you – shout and mingle.

Troubleshooting problems with the venue

You may arrive to find that things aren't the way you want them. Fixing them can be challenging. Here are some of the problems that may plague you:

SHARK ALERT! 'VENUE RELATED' PROBLEMS

- It isn't the room you asked for
- Room layout isn't what you wanted
- Refreshments and hospitality are inadequate
- The temperature is uncomfortable, either boiling hot or icy cold
- There are distractions (for example, construction work) going on outside the room.

It isn't the room you asked for

The reality is you might not get it. On the day be prepared to work with the rooms you have but take this up with the venue later, especially regarding cost.

Room layout isn't what you wanted

Get there early to check that the rooms have been set up correctly and try to iron out any problems in good time. Point out the problems and ask what can be done to resolve them. Don't lose your temper.

It may be that your allocated room contains furniture that cannot be moved around (for example, a large boardroom table). Try to get another room but accept it may not be possible and live with the consequences. If furniture can be moved, request help. Don't ask participants to move heavy furniture, as they may injure themselves. Position your equipment so that everyone can see clearly. Refer to Appendix B for choice of room layout.

Remember you may need to review your risk assessment, see Health and Safety in Chapter 3.

Refreshments and hospitality are inadequate

Have water on the tables: this also helps in case of late arrival of refreshments. If refreshments are late in arriving, try to be flexible in moving breaks to accommodate this. Break when the food/drink does arrive, as rumbling stomachs do nothing to aid concentration.

If your food hasn't arrived, the audience may be getting restless. They will almost certainly be clock-watching as lunchtime approaches and will appreciate your acknowledging that lunch is late: at least you're all hungry together! Chase up your venue contact, ask them to get back to you with news of progress and keep the audience informed.

The temperature is uncomfortable, either boiling hot or icy cold

To relieve the doziness and lethargy caused by very hot rooms, open windows or ask for fans to be provided if windows can't be opened (because of air conditioning systems). A cooler room keeps people more alert. If it's too cold, ask for heaters. If none are available request a supply of hot drinks.

There are distractions (for example, construction work) going on outside the room

Be assertive and insist that the noise stops. Your concession will be to signal when breaks are being taken so that external work can resume. Distractions outside your control (for example, traffic noise) have to be lived with.

The show must go on

The guidelines in this chapter won't prevent banana skins from appearing, but they will help you to skate confidently around them and keep your show on the road. Above all, it will be your professionalism and organisational expertise that people will remember. So whatever happens on the day, smile and act like the trouper you are.

9 *Icebreakers, Energisers and Team Exercises*

The following exercises have been designed for people to enjoy. Enjoyment is really important at an Away Day. Each of the four types of exercise has its own specific purpose:

Icebreakers break the ice, help people get into the spirit of the Day by breaking down barriers and allowing people to meet each other in a friendly, informal manner.

Energisers wake people up by encouraging them to be energetic in an enjoyable way for a few moments so that they can concentrate on what's happening next.

Team exercises exert great influence on the success of an Away Day. Why is this? They get results! They help teams to bond whilst tackling work-related tasks and as they are creative processes, people usually really enjoy them. People make decisions, develop plans or come to conclusions as a result of team exercises. A great example is our tried and tested team exercise *Flipping the Coin* which we frequently use to help teams make difficult decisions.

Individual exercises enhance self-learning. They are activities primarily designed to offer opportunities for personal reflection.

Examples of each are given below.

Please note that the participant material for these exercises may be photocopied for use in your training. Please make sure you include the 'Reproduced from ...' text on any copies that you make of these pages.

Icebreakers	Getting to Know You
	Hopes for the Day
	Mad Money
Energisers	Crocodiles
	Time for Tea
Team exercises	Adjectives for All
	Ask the Panel
	Flipping the Coin
	Papering the Plan
	Revelation Cards
Individual exercise	Building on our Strengths

Flexibility

Although we have recommended particular exercises for particular Days, many of them are interchangeable. Please feel free to use them as you think best suits your event, or even design your own.

Icebreaker: The 'Getting to Know You' game

Numbers: Unlimited
Overall time: 10 minutes

Purpose

The following icebreaker can be used as a light-hearted, low-risk exercise where strangers can get to know each other a little better. Our experience is that the stuffiest of people will play this and enjoy it. We have used this frequently at the beginning of large and international conferences.

Preparation

The information grid can easily be adapted to suit your type of audience or event. The information shown here was used most successfully at a conference for professors and experts on international drugs prevention policies.

If you don't need to change anything just photocopy the information grid overleaf, one for every participant.

Running the exercise

1 Get everyone's attention
2 Tell them how the exercise works
3 When someone shouts out that they have finished (that is, they have a name in each box) call the exercise to an end
4 Thank everyone and suggest that they may find out a bit more about some of the stories behind the answers during breaks and mealtimes.

How does it work?

Each person gets a copy of the grid and is asked to stand up and mingle amongst the whole group, finding individuals who have experienced one of the statements shown. The name of the person must then be written in that box. Only one name per box and every name must be different. As soon as a participant shouts 'bingo' or 'house' or 'finished' the game comes to an end and the grid is checked. If all the answers are correct, declare that participant the winner. A small prize might be offered but it is not necessary.

 ## SHARK ALERT! POTENTIAL PITFALLS

- Be careful to use criteria that suits your audience and won't upset or insult them because it is culturally, racially or sexually out of kilter.
- Give very clear instructions especially if many of your audience are working with English as a second language.
- Emphasise in your instructions that no name can be repeated on a grid. Participants must have 16 different names.
- Sometimes a person can find 16 names very quickly almost before the game seems to have warmed up. Congratulate the winner and tell them that you are looking for second and third place winners. This will give the game longer for its true purpose to happen.

The 'Getting to Know You' Game

Your instructions: find people who have experienced the statements in the boxes below. Write the person's name in the box that applies to them. No name must be repeated.

When you have a name in each box, shout 'bingo' or 'house' or 'finished'.

Has a child under 5 years old	Lives by the sea	Has spent time on national service	Wears glasses or contact lenses
Has worked in a restaurant	Has had at least one broken bone	Has visited London more than 3 times	Grows fruit and/ or vegetables
Has been to a rock/pop concert	Has eaten octopus	Has a bicycle	Is left handed
Doesn't eat meat	Keeps a pet	Is wearing blue	Has driven a truck or lorry

Remember to shout 'bingo' or 'house' when you are finished.

The 'Getting to Know You' Game (1 of 1)
Reproduced from *Legendary Away Days*,
by Karen Cooley and Kirsty McEwan, Gower, Aldershot.

Icebreaker: Hopes for the Day

Numbers: Unlimited
Overall time: Manage the exercise to last for up to 15 minutes

Purpose
To focus people's minds and get them engaged with the process of the Day.

Preparation
Have a supply of blank cards or slips of paper (approximately 12 cm by 15 cm).

Have two boxes to hold the cards or slips. The boxes should have a slit into which cards are posted, like a ballot box, so that participants are assured that there is no rigging or tampering taking place. One box should be clearly marked 'Hopes' and the other 'Concerns'.

Running the exercise
The facilitator introduces the exercise by asking each participant to take two cards or slips of paper. Explain that there are two ballot boxes: one for hopes, one for concerns.

> Ask: What are your hopes for the event?
>   What are your concerns about today?

Ask people to write their number one hope on one card and their number one concern on the other.

Allow 5 minutes maximum for thinking of ideas and noting them on the cards.

People move to the boxes as fast as possible and post their ideas into the relevant boxes. The facilitator collects the cards and reads them out whilst a participant scribes the ideas on a flipchart.

Addressing outstanding concerns
If the concerns haven't cropped up and been dealt with during the Day then they will need to be closed off at the end of the event so that people don't leave feeling their concerns have not been addressed.

You may not be able to resolve every concern on the Day and it is necessary to state this explicitly (perhaps in your introduction) so that people's expectations are not raised and then dashed.

Icebreaker: Mad Money

Numbers: Up to 12
Overall time: Up to 30 minutes

Purpose

To encourage participants to see one another as people as well as colleagues by learning more about each other as individuals in a supportive and fun way.

Preparation

You'll need:

- Supply of £10 notes in toy money
- Blank cards (approximately 12cm × 15cm)

Running the exercise

Divide the group into two or four teams of equal numbers depending on number of players. Explain that each participant is to share with their own team two facts about themselves that the others may not know – however one of the facts will be a lie. Only one is the truth. No questions may be asked.

Tell the groups that they are not to divulge which fact is the lie as this is the point of the exercise. Both facts must be non work-related. When everyone has disclosed their facts to their team the game may begin.

Step 1: Takes place within teams

Each person in team A considers what each of their own team-mates has said in turn. On a card they note the fact that they believe to be true about each person.

This card is *not* to be shown to their team-mates.

After everyone has spoken and completed their cards it is disclosure time and each individual reveals their 'truth' to their team (but *not* to the other team).

For each correct guess made, team members will be awarded £10 in toy money by the facilitator. Each individual notes how much 'money' they have made.

Step 2: Takes place between teams

By this point, team A knows only the truths about its own members. The same is true for team B – but this is about to change.

Next each of the members of team B says out loud to the other team their two facts (without revealing which in the lie). Team A then asks three questions of each member of team B (and teams C and D if you have four teams) to help them guess the true fact about them. Three questions in total may be directed at each member of team B. No exceptions! The situation is then reversed as members of team A each reveal their two facts to team B. Team B then asks three questions of each member of team A to help them guess the true fact about them. Three questions in total may be directed at each member of team A. No exceptions!

After two minutes for team debate about what they have heard, each team arrives at their team decision (that is, which is the true fact about *each person* in the other team).

Step 3: Disclosure time again!

This time team members reveal their own 'truth' to the other team.

The opposing team receives £10 toy money from the facilitator for every correct guess they made.

Debrief

- Who has more money – each individual or the team?
- Was the team more effective than individuals?
- Did it help being able to ask questions?
- What kinds of assumptions were made?
- How does this affect working in teams?

Note

Generally speaking, teams will have made more toy money than individuals. This is a useful exercise for emphasising the power of teamworking.

Energiser: Crocodiles

Numbers: Up to 30
Overall time: 15 minutes

Purpose

This is an energiser to use when participants have been working hard mentally but have been sitting for a long time with little physical freedom. Use this exercise when energy is low and there is obvious sleepiness or lethargy amongst the group. The purpose of this energiser is to wake everyone up, change the rhythm of the day and keep people alert. This will increase levels of participation.

We've used this game most successfully with groups of graduates who are attending a seminar on how their new company organises itself. Usually participants already know each other to some degree.

Preparation

You don't need any photocopies or special props for this game; just some space, some sheets of flipchart paper and a loud scary voice. You need to get the space ready before the participants come back to or into the room. You may need to allocate more 'crocodiles' (facilitators) depending on the size of the group and the length of time you want to spend on the exercise. We've played this with approximately 45 people and two 'crocodiles' and a ruthless adherence to the rules of being 'killed'.

Running the exercise

1 Prepare a space (you may need to move tables and chairs back to the sides of your room to make it safe for people to move about freely). A separate room could be used instead if you have access to one.
2 Scatter blank flipchart sheets on the floor. A ratio of about five sheets of flipchart paper for every ten people is recommended.
3 Invite everyone to participate and explain the game's instructions.
4 Be a crocodile, eliminate participants who are 'dead' and gradually remove 'islands'.
5 Declare the winner and applaud loudly.

How does it work?

Tell the participants that the flipchart sheets represent islands; islands of safety. The area between the islands is swampland in which they need to move about all the time going about their business ... until the facilitator shouts 'crocodiles'. Every participant has to jump onto a safe island, out of the way of the crocodiles (the facilitators). Anyone with any part of his or her anatomy still touching swampland in any way will be declared 'dead' and has to leave the game to become a spectator. Gradually withdraw the islands and break up some of the flipchart sheets too, leaving smaller pieces of paper. Do this gradually until there is only enough paper for one or two to stand on. Declare the last survivor as the winner.

SHARK ALERT! POTENTIAL PITFALLS AND SOME EXTRA OPPORTUNITIES

- Use this exercise when people know each other, at least a little. Or when the group is made up of people who are used to high energy or physical contact activities.
- Don't use this exercise if making a fool of themselves will be a big problem for your participants.
- Don't use this exercise if your participants will have serious issues about being physically touched in any way.
- Think carefully about the needs of any participant with movement difficulties (see 'Pitfalls' on page 65).
- Make sure the area where you play this game is made safe as it can get a little hectic.
- It is ideal to play this after lunch or at mid afternoon when people may be showing signs of tiredness.
- Make sure you play your role as a very scary crocodile with gusto. Some screaming and yelling will be good release for a sleepy team.
- Make sure you will not alarm or disturb other working groups nearby.

Energiser: Time for Tea

Numbers: As many as you like provided that everyone can see the items on the tea tray
Overall time: Allow 2 mins for viewing and 5 mins for feedback

Purpose

This is an energiser to use late in the Day, after the tea break, when people may be starting to feel listless and beginning to watch the clock. It is very useful with groups who don't know one another well as there is no element of personal disclosure involved – and we've found that by combining the note of competition with the notion of a tea break most people enjoy taking part in this game!

Preparation

You'll need:

- A tea tray
- 20 objects that have been used during the day
- Paper and pens.

Show the team a large tea tray that has been set out with 20 objects that have been used during the day. Include some 'teatime' items on the tray such as mugs, teaspoons and a packet of biscuits!

Also include items that will stimulate recollection of key learning points from the day. Be creative! Examples might include:

- Props that you may have used during the event so far
- If you have been practising brainstorming, include something that will remind people of the activity. Did you brainstorm '101 things to do with a paperclip?' Include a packet of paper clips. Did you brainstorm a workplace problem? Include any corporate literature that you can find about this project or issue – a magazine, a poster, or leaflets.

Running the Exercise

The group may view the tea tray for 2 minutes after which it is removed from sight.

They then have 5 minutes in which to agree the items on the tray before feeding back to the facilitator.

If they get all 20 items correct, you may want to award a team prize.

SHARK ALERT! POTENTIAL PITFALLS

- This is very obvious but just in case: this is not a good exercise for any team member with impaired vision.

Team exercise: Adjectives for All

Numbers: Unlimited although if there are more than 10 participants, people should sit
                with other people that they have worked with on the Day or know well.
Overall time: 10 minutes

Purpose
So that everyone receives a positive comment about themselves in order to boost their confidence and morale.

There are two versions of this exercise: an energetic version and a calm and reflective version.

Timing
Run this exercise at the end of a Day, just before evaluations are completed.

Preparation
For the energetic version, have a supply of hundreds of sticky labels. Each person could hand out up to ten labels to colleagues.

There is no preparation for the calm version.

Running the exercise
Ask everyone to think of a positive adjective for each person in their group such as 'hardworking', 'focused', 'friendly'. There is no qualification permitted, for example 'X is sometimes supportive, but not when they're busy'. Individuals may need clarification of someone's description of them and this should be given by way of an observed example from the Day or a recent piece of work.

For the energetic version, write the adjective on a sticky label (one adjective per label) and stick it onto each person for them to read when invited to do so. Advise individuals to stick their labels on people's arms and backs only, thus avoiding any embarrassment.

The facilitator allows 8 minutes for thinking and writing labels, and a further 2 minutes for running around sticking the labels.

Invite people to read what's been said about them and then close the Day.

For the calm version, each team member notes their thoughts about their colleagues and is prepared to say out loud one positive word or phrase about each colleague at their table. No discussion is to take place about the comment. Individuals may wish to discuss it after the event; this will be up to them. On hearing any negativity ask the participant to desist immediately and find a positive comment.

As soon as everyone has made and received a comment, close the Day with thanks.

 SHARK ALERT! POTENTIAL PITFALLS
- Make sure that there are no hazards in the way, such as furniture. You don't want people to risk injuring themselves or others.
- For the calm version, participants remain seated and one adjective per person is spoken aloud.
- If you choose the calm version, ensure that you end the Day immediately after ending the exercise so people aren't left looking at each other and potentially feeling rather embarrassed having just received compliments from those around them.

Team exercise: Ask the Panel

Numbers: Unlimited
Overall time: Two options. A shorter exercise of 30 minutes or lengthen it into a session of
                up to one hour.

Purpose
To allow participants to ask constructive questions whilst remaining anonymous

Timing
People need to have heard the speeches first so that they have some knowledge on which to base their questions. Use a coffee break to allow people to think about, write and post their questions.

Preparation
Have a large number of cards or slips of paper placed on the tables so that participants can easily find them and write out their questions.

Have a box or boxes to hold the cards or slips. The boxes should have a slit into which cards are posted, like a ballot box, so that participants are assured that there is no rigging or tampering taking place.

Make up a panel of 2–6 people, ensuring that there is a mix of knowledge, experience, authority and charisma.

Running the exercise
The facilitator introduces the exercise and explains the purpose of having the box. Allocates time for question writing. Collects the slips in the boxes and delivers them to the panel for random selection and answering.

The facilitator explains the amount of time available for answering questions and hands over to the panel to begin.

For the 30 minute version, the facilitator takes the ballot box into the audience for ten randomly chosen questions for the panel to answer. Obviously if they need any more questions take another as required and if too much discussion ensues, then promise that some of that discussion will be followed up outside of the event if no further time is available during the Day. If you feel that the discussion is really valuable to the group then re-jig the programme to suit the team's needs.

For the longer version use exactly the same process. You will have more time available for questions and in-depth discussion.

The facilitator will call time at the end of the session.

Team exercise: Flipping the Coin

Numbers: Up to 20
Overall time: 35 minutes

Purpose

This exercise is used in decision-making activities, where it reveals the advantages and disadvantages of the choices on offer that may not have been immediately apparent.

Preparation

The facilitator sets up the exercise by arranging flipchart paper and pens around the room so that team members can record their initial thoughts.

Running the exercise

Display the choices on offer to the whole group and ask each individual to select their top three choices from the list.

Divide the group into pairs. Ask the pairs to swap their top choices. Each participant then lists the advantages and disadvantages of their partner's choices. Allow 10 minutes per person. At the end of this time, the facilitator calls the group back together.

As the debrief, ask the following recommended questions:

- Has anybody changed their minds as a result of the exercise?
- Has anybody adapted an idea as a result of discussion?
- Were any new ideas discovered?

Allow maximum 10 minutes for discussion about the questions.

Team exercise: Papering the Plan

Numbers: Up to 30
Overall time: 1 to 1½ hours

Purpose
So that people can see how a plan might work in a logical and chronological order. To start making the plan become a reality for the group.

Preparation
A large roll of wall lining paper is necessary. The facilitator sticks the paper onto the wall around the room to give participants a blank canvas to write on.

Draw a single dark line horizontally around the top of the paper and mark off time slots such as months or weeks depending on the duration of the project.

Running the exercise
Start with one or two milestones that are 'givens' which will affect the team over the period of the project. These should be organisational or whole team milestones. The team needs to write them onto the paper.

The next step is to add their own department or smaller group milestones (hopefully people will be working at different physical points on the paper because their roles will be called upon at different points of the project).

As the group slows down, call time on the writing process and ask the whole group to reflect and study the plan so far. Ask them the following questions:

- Is this plan in the right order?
- Are we doing the right things?
- Have we missed anything out?

If there is anything to change, amend as per response. Then start looking at the plan in more detail. Ask the group to think about:

- Resources needed to implement the plan
- Skills and development needed
- What support do they need (allies, champions)?
- Contingency plans and time
- What do they personally need to do to make the plan work?
- Impacts: what impact will their activities have on others (and vice versa). What do they need to do about this?
- What are their key priorities?
- What parts of the plan need to happen so that other parts of the plan can happen (the critical path points)?

The facilitator asks the group to select which categories are the most important at the moment for them to work on.

Once this is established and the group has thought about the issues, they can apply more detail to the plan, for example who needs what specific resource? What funding is required to make this part of the plan happen? The facilitator asks them to consider the following two issues:

- What are the key action points that will make the plan happen?
- What needs to be done to overcome any identified problems or barriers?

The group creates an action point list, including their suggested ways of overcoming the barriers.

Reward the team for such hard work with lunch or an icebreaker such as *Crocodiles* (see Chapter 9).

Team exercise: Revelation Cards

Numbers: No limit
Overall time: 45 minutes

Purpose
To get people to express clearly what they found enjoyable and beneficial about working with each other on a project.

Preparation
Make up a set of about 15 cards for each group at the event. Each set is identical and is made up of cards (15cm x 12cm approximately). Put each of the following statements (or your own selection) onto a separate card:

- What did you learn the most about whilst working together?
- What did you learn about yourself?
- What was the funniest thing that happened?
- What was your greatest contribution to this group?
- Who did you admire and why?
- What was the greatest challenge?
- Who was the most supportive to you?
- How did you support your colleagues?
- What kept the team together when the going got tough?
- What was the best thing about the team?
- What was the most surreal moment?
- What did you learn from each team member?
- What do you think other team members learned from you and how do you know?
- What one word or expression will stay with you about this team?
- What will you miss most about this team?

Substitute your own questions if desired but try not to be negative.

How this works
Divide your team into small groups (approximately four to six people per team).

Give each group a set of cards placed face down in the centre of the table. One team member takes a card and reads the question on the card out loud. The same person answers the question out loud and passes the card to the person on their left who then gives their answer and so on round the team until all have answered that question.

The next person then picks another card and the process is repeated until all the cards have been used.

If people have tackled this exercise from a heartfelt perspective they may have been quite moved by the experience. When ending the exercise the facilitator needs to emphasise the key themes that have emerged and show appreciation for the group's revelations.

Individual exercise: Building on our Strengths

Overall time: About 15 minutes

Purpose
This is a self-assessment exercise to assist with positive thinking and to reinforce and acknowledge our own personal strengths.

Preparation
None.

Running the exercise
Each participant has an assessment form. Ask each participant to carry out the steps on the handout.

Building on our Strengths

1 Sit on your own and jot down a few things under each heading below.

2 Get into pairs. Take turns to go through your list and try saying each one in a straightforward, calm manner. The other person can help you do this.

3 At the end of the conversation at step 2, choose one thing you feel comfortable about saying to the whole group:

'Some of my strengths and skills are …'

For example, being a good parent, managing my budget, supporting colleagues when they are feeling down, coaching my team members.

I am   ....

I am   ....

I am   ....

'Some things I like about myself are … '

For example, my honesty and openness, my jokes, my values

I like   ....

I like   ....

I like   ....

'Positive things others say about me are … '

For example, reliable, good fun, caring, intelligent, assertive

Others say I am   ....

Others say I am   ....

Others say I am   ....

Building on our Strengths (1 of 1)
Reproduced from *Legendary Away Days*,
by Karen Cooley and Kirsty McEwan, Gower, Aldershot.

THREE *The Legendary Away Days*

Introduction

The following Legendary Away Days are especially designed for you to use in a wide range of circumstances. Each Day has a straightforward outline plan, a step-by-step guide with plenty of practical advice on how to design and run your events. It even includes potential pitfalls, highlighted by a shark symbol that will help prevent you getting into deep water.

You are in control of your team events. We want you to tailor each Day to make it highly relevant and special for your teams. So why not pick and choose from the plethora of advice we offer to customise the experience for your audience? Choosing is easy. We have even provided a reality check for each Day so that you can be sure that you are using the right Day. It's headed *Key question: What is this really about?*

We've made it easy for you to get started without delay, achieve results, receive excellent feedback and be recognised for your success. A brief reminder: please always take a look at the sharks, they are there for a reason.

Although we have used the term Away Day throughout the book, this has been largely for consistency. You may of course only need to run a half-day event or extend to two (or more) days if team size and quantity of work demand this.

There are several roles mentioned in Part Three and here we explain what they mean:

We see a 'sponsor' as someone who has responsibility for the team and possibly many more teams. They may not be this team's direct line manager but a more senior manager with a strong interest in team development and results.

We see a 'team leader' as someone who is either the team's direct line manager or their project manager. This person is likely to be keenly interested in the ongoing success of the team and its development, being close to the team on a daily basis.

We see a 'facilitator' as someone who acts as the team's support for the Day. They are either an experienced internal or external professional or someone who has a great interest in helping with process and group development. Although they might be part of the team, keeping neutral could be an issue for them and the team.

For simplicity we have chosen to address you directly on many occasions irrespective of the role you are in. In this way you will receive our guidance in the most accessible form.

A note about consensus-reaching: firstly, many think that reaching consensus in groups is a must but, although it is the ideal, it is notoriously difficult to achieve. Don't pressurise yourself too much. There are other ways around this issue which are mentioned throughout the days, for example voting systems, prioritising and pro's and con's. Formal and informal selection systems are shown throughout, for example *Ranking and Rating* (Appendix G) and for an informal process see Chapter 14 The Consultation Day.

Another important way of helping people towards consensus is to offer them strict timescales for debate. Ensure that each person has had an opportunity to say their piece, after which the group seeks to achieve consensus. If this is not possible within the timescale, an alternative decision-making process must be adopted (see Chapter 16 The Decision Making Day).

10 *The Celebration Day*

What is a Celebration Day?

A DEFINITION

This is a Day designed to focus on success. It is a time for a group to acknowledge, through the ritual of celebration, that they have achieved something special together.

This type of event can also be used by managers to thank their ongoing teams for all their hard work and give them a time and space to affirm their strengths and achievements.

There is a difference between a good party and a Celebration Day, although a Celebration Day will certainly have elements of both. What is the difference? Whereas parties are often about leaving your work behind, a Celebration Day is about putting some aspects of work into acute focus.

By building into the Day a sequential process including a period of time set aside for people to express their feelings, you are recognising that some people will be saying 'goodbye' to one another with all the emotions that this involves. For some this will be akin to a sense of grief. For organisations to invest in a Celebration Day, they need to see some return and this will often come in the form of team members being ready to start new work fully motivated, without the weight of hankering after their old 'great team' because they have been able to say goodbye in a healthy and happy way.

When to use a Celebration Day

- When a project is over
- When a difficult transition has been accomplished
- When groups have been through a difficult time and have struggled but survived
- When there is a good excuse for a celebration (such as Christmas or mid-summer) which will drive motivation levels up to sustain an organisation for months to come
- When there are profits and plenty of resources to celebrate with
- When a large piece of work has been won
- When there are great things to celebrate such as a successful and wanted merger
- When leaders want to end a group's working relationship in a healthy and positive way
- When groups need to be motivated to accept that their present roles have changed and they need to move on.

Key question: What is this really about?

We have found (as facilitators and managers) that purposefully bringing everyone together to concentrate on the emotional and practical experience that has been shared over a period of time helps teams come to terms with the often hidden impact of, for example:

- ending projects
- team secondments
- the work of a task force
- reorganisation.

Desired outcomes: What's happened as a result of the Day?

- People are motivated to work hard for new goals with their new colleagues.
- People have had a great opportunity to network and now know each other better.
- People accept the ending of one work team and feel more positive about the formation of the new team.
- People have reconciled their sadness about moving away from colleagues or vice versa and are positively philosophical about it.
- Attitudes about the organisation are good; it is felt to be a sound team, department or company to work in.

SHARK ALERT! POTENTIAL PITFALLS

- There is animosity amongst the group that has not evaporated prior to the end of the project and creates an 'atmosphere' at the event.
- Participants take full advantage of the alcohol that is available at the event and many become drunk and irresponsible.
- Participants celebrate the night before the event and many are not very bright and energetic on the morning of the event due to hangovers.
- Some people don't attend the event because of bad feeling between them and others or yourself as leader.
- The venue is not suitable for celebrating, as they don't approve of noise or rowdiness.
- This is a great opportunity for a leader to give a stirring speech and raise motivation to very high levels. It should not be an opportunity missed.
- If leaders aren't generous about their thanks, this will be noticed by participants and can counteract all the effort put into celebrating.
- Tailor your celebration so that you can include everyone, for example by demonstrating sensitivity to those who don't drink alcohol.

How? The approach

Step 1   Welcome and introductions
Step 2   Illustrate the achievements
Step 3   Capture the essence of the team

Step 4   Keep in touch
Step 5   Tie up loose ends
Step 6   The party

Broad outline for the Day

STEP 1: WELCOME AND INTRODUCTIONS

Objectives for Step 1
- To ensure that everyone knows each other (or at least those at the table they are sitting at if there are a large number of people at the event).
- To offer background information as to why this Day is happening.
- To ensure that everyone knows the process for the Day and what is expected of them including the ground rules for the event.

The leader or sponsor opens the Day by giving a brief outline as to what has led to the event and explains what will be happening.

The facilitator discusses with the group what is required of everyone for it to be successful and enjoyable (see Chapter 4 for the setting, agreeing and use of ground rules). They also confirm that they will be checking throughout the Day to ensure that any concerns are noted and added to an 'issues sheet' (flipchart paper on the wall).

Two particular ground rules for a Celebration Day are:

- To enjoy yourself but respect others' boundaries
- To minimise negativity.

If there are any team members who are unknown to others, initiate an icebreaker exercise. If all team members are known to each other, we suggest using an energiser to create a fun atmosphere. Chapter 9 has examples of both types of exercise.

STEP 2: ILLUSTRATE THE ACHIEVEMENTS

Objectives for Step 2
- To ensure that everyone shares in recalling and presenting their 'highlights' of team achievement over the appropriate period of time.
- To ensure that all the achievements are understood.
- To reach shared conclusions about the benefits of their efforts to the organisation.
- To highlight some individual contributions.

This is an important session as it reminds each participant about their contribution to achievements. It is also a time to highlight one or two special contributions although the main spotlight is on the team as a whole.

We recommend a three-stage process to achieve the best results and maximise people's chances of enjoyment.

1 Form groups (up to ten participants – divide into two groups, and over ten – put into a number of small groups). Allow half an hour for the groups to think about their achievements so far on their project and help each other to draw out their recollections of what has happened. Tell the groups to capture their lists on flipchart paper and include a mix of light-hearted and weighty achievements. Each sub-group presents back their findings to the whole group.

2 Keep the groups as they are, allocate a further half hour, and ask them to create an image, structure or jingle that represents their findings. Suggest that the representation is in the style of the product or service offered by the organisation:

   - advertising agencies could write an advert extolling the benefits of the achievements of the team.
   - an engineering organisation could create a structure that represents all the achievements of the team, for example a very solid structure to indicate how solid the team has been.

   Each group decides who will be their spokesperson. This person invites suggestions from the rest of their group about who, in their opinion, has made a special contribution to the project or work. (Special can mean what the group decides – the most inventive, the most hardworking, the most fun.) A maximum of one third of the total allocated time should be spent on this part of the task.

3 Each group presents their creation, and their nomination for the *special contributor*, to the rest of the participants who are encouraged to cheer and applaud.

STEP 3: CAPTURING THE ESSENCE OF THE TEAM

Objectives for Step 3
- To get people to clearly express what they found enjoyable and beneficial about working with each other.
- To get people to express these thoughts from a personal perspective.

SHARK ALERT! POTENTIAL PITFALLS

- Many teams can get tangled up in seeing the negative from an experience rather than the positive. Discourage negative comment unless it is truly constructive with a positive meaning.
- Avoid referring to this exercise as an emotional exercise as this may unnerve some participants who will be reluctant to express themselves in this way. Let it evolve naturally instead of forcing it.
- There is a risk that some participants will not take this step seriously (as a way of denying their own emotional responses and avoiding revealing those responses to others). By remaining serious and expressing a genuine belief in the process, the facilitator will help others to offer their honest views.

Ask the groups to carry out a reflective exercise based on a series of questions (see Chapter 9 for *Revelation Cards* exercise). Now that the group members have had an opportunity to express their feelings about working together as a team and confirmed what they really enjoyed, the facilitator summarises the exercise and looks to capitalise on the energy in the room by introducing Step 4.

STEP 4: KEEPING IN TOUCH

Objectives for Step 4
- To facilitate the process by which team members can network if they wish.
- To hand over responsibility to the team for maintaining contact with each other.

SHARK ALERT! POTENTIAL PITFALLS

The team may wish you to keep responsibility for their networking. However strong the temptation, resist the urge and find two or more people to hand it over to before you leave the Day.

The facilitator asks the team if they want to stay in contact. If they say 'yes', ask each group to explore how this could happen and ask them to present back their views to the whole team. Try and get consensus on the method otherwise the opportunity will have passed and from now on it will be up to individual team members to go forward as they think best.

STEP 5: TYING UP LOOSE ENDS

Objectives for Step 5
- To ensure that there are no outstanding concerns or issues.
- To close the serious part of the Day.
- To link seamlessly into the social part of the event.

The facilitator will acknowledge any outstanding issues if they exist, having identified them throughout the Day by frequent referral to the team.

Remember to ask people to complete their evaluation sheets. See Part Four for information on evaluation, and Appendices J–N for example evaluation forms.

The facilitator says a few positive words about their experience of working with the team and the team leader reiterates this. The team leader also thanks everybody for their contribution, both to the team effort and to today's event and declares that the party is now on. Everyone is invited!

STEP 6: THE PARTY

Objective for the party
- For people to enjoy themselves

Some examples of the social part of the event could be:
- A meal in a restaurant
- A stand-up buffet with opportunity to mingle and chat
- A full-on party with music, dancing, entertainment and themed décor
- The team provides its own entertainment (sketches, singing, music, pantomime)
- An activity (paintballing, a visit to the races, sporting competition, theatre visit)
- A themed ball (often a midsummer ball)
- A quiz with prizes.

... and finally

People will take a view of you as a team leader by the way that you interact with others at an event such as this. We recommend that you mix with everyone (not just your closest friends or other managers in the team). Show your interest in others (including those who you don't regularly work with) as this will be remembered and will win you respect as a leader.

RECOMMENDED ROOM LAYOUT

If you are using a large venue, sit people in Cabaret style at round tables for increased participation and comfort. Try not to have glaring bright lights as this detracts from the informal atmosphere you are trying to create. If the team is small in number (up to 10) a private lounge area with sofas and armchairs might be a very pleasant and enjoyable setting. See Appendix B for choice of room layouts.

11 *The Challenge of Change Day*

What is a Challenge of Change Day?

A DEFINITION

There are two main types of change; strategic (the big picture) and operational (the day to day).

Strategic change is about organisation-wide change. It is also usually about the long-term. The words frequently used around strategic change tend to relate to company values and culture, innovation and development, visions and missions.

Operational change is about what impacts the business or organisation in the short-term; those factors that will have an immediate effect on the day-to-day processes and procedures. In the short term the impact of operational change can far outweigh that of strategic change, as adjustments in the familiar disturb us.

EXAMPLES OF BOTH TYPES OF CHANGE

- Where a need for efficiency dictates a possible change in roles or location.
- Where there is a need for a shift or new position in work focus.
- Where a request for changes in environmental factors is demanded, for example relocation or a different use of existing building space.
- When teams need to respond to external changes forced upon the organisation or department.
- Where there is a need for a change in priorities due to pressure from the external market place or legislation, such as new health and safety regulations being introduced.
- When the facts of a situation are so constraining that change must happen in order for the organisation or the team to survive.
- When change is created on purpose to challenge the status quo.
- Where there is a change in customer requirements that necessitates a rethink about existing services and products.
- With the appointment of a new leader with desires to change the way work is carried out, or where a new chief executive is recruited partly because of their different vision for the future.
- When shareholders choose to restrict the board's innovative spending activities and redirect them to cut costs and concentrate on core business which may mean changing peoples' roles and work functions.
- When there is an economic requirement to substantially reduce costs.

When to use a Challenge of Change Day

This is a Day to use where you need to implement change. One thing is for sure; if you don't take care to plan how to 'sell' the benefits of change to people and persuade them of the opportunities on offer, you could find very little support for your implementation plans. You could even be unintentionally setting up the conditions for people to deliberately or unconsciously sabotage your change programme. Individuals react to change in different ways depending on their personalities and personal circumstances. Those who object to change need to be treated carefully. The key to successful change management is good planning; make an Away Day like this part of your planned programme.

Key question: What is this really about?

This is about understanding how to manage change effectively and to treat people with respect. If you don't consult, you won't get commitment. Without commitment you risk your carefully laid plans being undermined and misunderstood. This could manifest itself through denial, disinterest or withdrawal of goodwill. You will want to keep your supporters 'on-side' and win over any doubters to your purpose. Consultation has been proven over and over again to encourage willing engagement with change issues. Even where people already know about proposed changes in principle, the Day gives them a chance to come to terms with the changes for themselves and to appreciate the need for sensitivity in encouraging their own teams to be more accepting. Do you, as the manager, really have the answers to every technical or team relationship question that may be asked? Perhaps your team is able to make a critical and intelligent input into the design of the change process?

SHARK ALERT! POTENTIAL PITFALLS

- Not taking account of the emotional response of participants and expecting them to move forward into decision-making and action planning when they are not yet ready.
- Not consulting to get their views.
- Participants becoming antagonised either by the prospect of change or the details of the implementation.
- Threatening participants if they don't agree to the changes; an unfortunate Armageddon technique based on 'do it or else' which just alienates, saddens and angers team members.
- Individual or small groups attempting to hijack the Day by ruining the event, for example by forming opposing factions.
- Not providing support after the event for individuals who are more reflective and possibly more upset than others.
- In their own enthusiasm for change managers can fail to recognise the lack of commitment of their teams.
- Assuming that participants can take in the information about proposed change at the same pace as you. Ensure that there is enough time for participants to reflect and think through the change proposals. Help them by asking facilitative questions that encourage them to concentrate on what the change will mean to them personally and to their teams.

Desired outcomes: What's happened as a result of the Day?

- People are still able to express their views and know that they will be listened to.
- Managers value the opinions and contributions of their teams.
- Those who wanted to have been able to express their concerns and fears.
- Discussion and any dissent have been handled in an open, honest and adult manner.
- People feel more involved in the process and as a result are more likely to accept, or at least consider, change.
- People make a conscious decision to align their behaviour with the new change being striven for.
- People feel as though their technical expertise has been sought.
- The best of the group's ideas will have been meshed into the plan.
- Many people have been won over or are no longer disgruntled by this change.
- People feel as though they are an integral part of the design process.
- People are sharing the inconvenience or even pain of change with each other and not dealing with it in isolation.
- Change is implemented successfully because the plan worked.
- The team has moved on and is busying itself with present duties and not dwelling on the past.
- The team may even be preparing for the next step in your change process.

How? The approach

Step 1   Welcome and introductions
Step 2   Background to the Day and presentation of the proposed change
Step 3   Reactions to the proposed change
Step 4   Development of commitment
Step 5   Design of the change process plan
Step 6   Confirm action plan and close the Day

Broad outline for the Day

STEP 1: WELCOME AND INTRODUCTIONS

Objectives for Step 1
- To set people's expectations for the event
- To set the desired tone and atmosphere
- To introduce all the contributors for the Day.

The team leader welcomes all present and introduces the Day. There may be a sense of apprehension and even anxiety, if people know that changes are going to be announced at the Day. It is important for the leader to set the right tone and create an atmosphere of being 'up front' and honest with participants. Managers are actively demonstrating that they care enough about the opinions of their staff to spend time consulting with them.

All the main contributors (speakers, facilitators, helpers) are introduced to the group.

If your audience is less than 30 strong, we would recommend that you invest a little time helping that group get to know one another so that they can offer each other support.

With a larger group the logistics become more difficult and you may wish to bypass the introductory exercises in favour of syndicate work.

STEP 2: BACKGROUND TO THE DAY AND PRESENTATION OF THE PROPOSED CHANGE

Objectives for Step 2

- To ensure that the reasons for the proposed change are clear and rational and that the team understand what is driving the need for the change.
- To ensure that the background to the proposed change and the full proposal are related to the audience by a respected senior person.
- To reassure people that as much as possible will be done to accommodate their concerns and needs.
- To check that everyone clearly understands the outcomes required from the proposed change.

It is best if the leader explains the reasons driving the need for change in rational and yet passionate terms. Passion or heart-felt enthusiasm can be motivating. Ensure that the message is sincere; false and incongruous behaviour will be recognised quickly and as a result the message may be rejected.

It is often hard for leaders to give their team 'difficult' news and it is tempting for those presenting bad news to detach themselves from it by blaming the organisation or others. To lead people through change successfully you will need to take them along with you in such a way that they believe that you believe it is the best thing to do in the circumstances.

The change outcomes need to be important to your team members and not just to you and the organisation. Ensure that the change outcomes are described in ways that make them attractive to the audience. The more desirable each outcome, the more likely people are to adopt behaviours that you want them to adopt and that are likely to lead to those outcomes.

STEP 3: REACTIONS TO THE PROPOSED CHANGE

Objectives for Step 3

- To ensure that people have an opportunity to express their views.
- To ensure that people have a process and place that is safe for them to share their concerns with you and each other.
- To show participants that they have been heard and their concerns and ideas have been noted for consideration.

Giving participants time and an acceptable process by which to express their fears and concerns about the proposed change will hopefully reduce resistance. This is a critical step in any change programme and shows that you care about people and how they feel. It also allows everyone time to begin coming to terms with the change. By talking to one another they will realise that they are not alone in having concerns about the change and how it is likely to affect them.

It is important that you, as leader, and your facilitator if you have one are on hand to field any questions that people may have.

STEP 4: DEVELOPMENT OF COMMITMENT

Objectives for Step 4
- To establish what would help participants become committed to the change.
- To ensure that appropriate support is available.
- To address fears.
- To create a shared vision.
- To manage resistance.

Increase commitment by involving everyone in the change programme. Discuss and agree what training will be required for the development of any new skills that may be required to carry out the change programme or any new roles that it has created. Explain to everyone, in a way that they will fully understand, how the change is likely to affect them. They should already know why the change needs to be made from Step 2. Avoid confrontation but be sympathetic as most of us don't like moving from positions of comfort into the unknown.

Overcome resistance by addressing fears and preventing disruptive reaction and behaviour. Resistance surfaces because people may be fearful about loss of control or power; the worry about potentially increased workloads; changes in skills and knowledge required to do new jobs; or through the sheer misunderstanding about what will happen to them.

When addressing fears, it is important that you don't infer that there is nothing to worry about when in reality there may well be, for example, future job cuts or cost cuts. Be realistic and truthful; people will never trust you again if you lie or omit information (even if you are well meaning). People who work for you and with you can only make the best choices for themselves when they have all the facts that are available at the time.

Make sure *everyone* has had an opportunity to say how they feel and what their concerns and views are about the change. Resistance can be overcome by:

- Involving
- Training
- Developing a shared vision of the future
- Communicating constantly to keep everyone informed of progress or changes to plans
- Avoiding confrontation
- Addressing concerns as they arise
- Explaining the reasons for changes
- Being sympathetic
- Explaining plans and outcomes in ways that people can understand without being patronising
- Acknowledging reactions and feelings.

Reactions to change process
There is a useful process frequently employed that helps us understand the different reactions to change. This process is also used to understand how we, as humans, travel through grief as one of the most impacting changes to happen to us. It suggests that we are likely to go through the following phases and it is hoped that we don't get stuck in any of them.

1 Shock of imposed information
2 Disbelief and denial at the change
3 Depression
4 Gradual acceptance of change
5 Resolution (a way of behaving differently from before the change happened to us). This is an indication that change has been fully assimilated.

Make sure you announce where and how further support is available in order to help people through the passage of change. A good way is to tell everyone that they can come and see you later for confidential discussion. You could also set up other support mechanisms, such as external facilitators and consultants who will be neutral, or engage the organisation's skilled Human Resources support team to counsel or talk through worries with anyone who wants to. The word 'counsel' may put people off by inferring that they can't cope. Try saying 'support' instead.

STEP 5: DESIGN OF THE CHANGE PROCESS PLAN

Objectives for Step 5
- To develop a plan with the team (if this is appropriate)
- To ensure that everyone understands the plan
- To ensure that expert views have been taken into account
- To consult the team on their views of the plan.

Planning means identifying what needs to happen so that the team can get from one point to another. It also means taking account of the problems and opportunities that may occur and anticipating further objections and resistances. Create a step-by-step plan to manage them. You may need an external facilitator on the Day to help you manage any negative responses in an objective, neutral way as you move through Steps 4 and 5.
      A recommended planning change process is to:

1 Analyse the nature of the change (anticipate pitfalls, the scale of the change needed, the resources that will probably be required).
2 Create a programme plan for the change and manage it much like a project. Have the end in mind and be clear about what it involves. Devise specific plans for the resources and the communication aspects of the programme, for example what you will need to say to stakeholders.
3 Track the plan to keep it on schedule and manage any unexpected obstacles which crop up.

The most important aim of change management is to gain commitment for proposed plans so make very sure that everyone fully understands the expected outcomes, the objectives and the plan itself.
      Ask team members for their views, using their expertise in planning and implementation to ensure that everything has been thought of. The more you consult the more people will become engaged with the process. Ask for their help, flatter them with regard to their skills and knowledge and ask for advice and support.

If the proposals have met with little resistance and the team is positive, why not ask them to support you and assist in creating the implementation plan? This way they have the advantage and benefits of designing it to suit themselves.

There may, however, be circumstances where you will want the plan designed carefully by yourself and will need to impose the process, for example when working on a downsizing plan.
Step 6: Confirm action plans and close the Day

Objectives for Step 6

- To ensure that all the action points are clear and recorded.
- To remind everyone of the support mechanisms that have been set up.
- To close the Day on a positive but realistic note.

As leader, thank everyone for their honesty in sharing their concerns and also thank them for any constructive ideas. Make sure that the team knows what your action points are and that you are committing to do something too.

Reassure everyone that you will do your best to keep them up to date with progress on the change programme. Remind them that you are available and receptive to anyone who wishes to talk to you privately.

Relate what will happen to all the action points, including yours.

It is important that everyone knows that there will be a follow-up of some sort, for example a meeting or an e-mail. Tell them when this will happen. Make sure that it does! It proves to people that you, as leader, are 'on the ball', leading from the front and that you care about them.

It is important that you evaluate people's initial reaction to the Day. If it has been negative you may need to carry out some remedial work very quickly. Remember evaluation is not just about a 'happy sheet' but also about gleaning deeper reactions and measuring how successful the change is over time. See Part Four for more detail about evaluation, and Appendices J–N for a selection of evaluation forms.

RECOMMENDED ROOM LAYOUT

Go for Cabaret or Conference style, with syndicate rooms if there are more than 30 people there. Ensure that your venue is suitable for people to feel safe to talk to each other. A range of syndicate rooms or round tables or cabaret style seating in a large room would suffice. See Appendix B for choice of room layouts.

12 *The Conference Day*

What is a Conference Day?

A DEFINITION

A Conference Day is an opportunity for communicating and sharing information with a group of colleagues. Often formal in structure and tone, a Conference Day offers a chance to gather together significant numbers of people and invite them to hear and understand matters of vital importance to the organisation.

The chief focus of the Day will be determined by the most senior team in the relevant area of the business; for example for a major new product launch it would be the sales and marketing directors. Attendees will be invited to ask questions and contribute their thoughts and opinions in open session, however the format of the Day will be tightly controlled by the senior team. Make opportunities available for further comment to take place away from the conference floor at a later time.

Conference Days vary in theme from a motivational, cheerful sales conference to a Day that has been called to announce corporate cutbacks or downsizing and redundancies. The outline of the Day will be tailored to reflect the mood of the event. The role of the facilitator (if you are using one) will be different from other Days, as there is less need for participant interaction and a greater need for co-ordinating progress, rather as a conductor would control and encourage an orchestra. The emphasis may concentrate on 'what is being told' rather than consultation.

When to use a Conference Day

- When it is time for colleagues to renew their sense of belonging and commitment to the organisation.
- When there is an exciting and/or important message to give to the team.
- When there is interesting information to be shared.
- If there is a new product or campaign being launched.
- Prior to a corporate acquisition or merger.
- When the most senior members of the team want or need to be visible.
- At the start of a major project.
- When the top team needs or wants to share its vision with the rest of the organisation.
- When the message needs to be delivered in a consistent format at the same time to large numbers of people.
- When the top team believes that people are becoming 'disconnected' and no longer feel part of the organisation.

Key question: What is this really about?

Of all the tools at the disposal of senior team members, the Conference Day is probably the most formal and useful. Its very existence sends out the message that 'there is very important information to give'. Although the term 'conference' literally means 'meeting for discussion', the Conference Day is more likely to be used by the top team to deliver a predetermined message to employees in easily recognisable corporate language in order to inform, inspire and rally them for the future.

 ## SHARK ALERT! POTENTIAL PITFALLS

- Be certain that there is a sensible reason for holding the Conference Day. You are asking significant numbers of people to spend time away from work at considerable cost. Can you justify this?
- Ensure that there is 'buy in' from the top team. Senior members of the team will be expected to make an appearance at a Conference Day and it will be embarrassing (as well as undermining to the sponsor) if none of them appear.
- This is a key opportunity to share information: don't miss it by failing to plan a well-scheduled running order.
- Check that there will be opportunities for participants to offer their thoughts and opinions throughout the event. Even where a serious message is being given, people will want to have their say. Control this impulse but don't suffocate it.
- Don't let the Day degenerate into a moaning session about the state of the organisation. Stay focused.
- Failure to make the presentation compelling will result in a bored audience.
- Make sure that everyone feels involved throughout the Day. The danger with larger-scale events is that those at the back of the auditorium feel disconnected from what is going on at the front, while the 'in crowd' sit at the front and own the Day. The Day belongs to everyone: so don't shut them out.

Desired outcomes: What's happened as a result of the Day?

- People feel that top management is aware of their existence.
- People feel more valued.
- People will discuss what they have heard and objectively assess its impact on themselves and the organisation.
- If the key message was optimistic and buoyant people will be motivated to achieve higher levels of performance.
- If the key message was stark and grim people will feel that at least they know the worst. They have been trusted with the truth, not kept in the dark.
- People will discuss the Day's news around the workplace.
- People will be animated and eager to get started on new projects.
- People will believe that the top team are in control and running the organisation well.

How? The approach

Step 1   Welcome and introductions
Step 2   Setting the scene and sharing the message
Step 3   Comments and questions from the floor
Step 4   Members of the top team define and explain what they see as the next steps
Step 5   Confirm follow-up and close the Conference.

Broad outline for the Day

STEP 1: WELCOME AND INTRODUCTIONS

Objectives for Step 1
- To set people's expectations of the Day, give background to the Day and agree ground rules.
- To alleviate people's concerns if the news is not going to be as bad as they fear.
- To create positive energy where the impetus of the Day is on motivation.
- To introduce the main contributors to the Day. In larger organisations the top team may be just names to many of the audience.

The sponsor welcomes participants and introduces the day. There will be a sense of anticipation or apprehension depending on the circumstances forming the backdrop of the Day and the manner of the sponsor needs to be sensitive to this in their welcome and introduction. They should give a broad outline of the main message that needs to be heard during the Day, but not give all the detail at this time.

A suggested icebreaker to use at a Conference Day is *Getting to know you* (see Chapter 9 for details of how to run this activity).

The sponsor indicates how the Day will be conducted. Although extensive ground rules will not need to be set for a Conference Day, general comments about how attendees are expected to conduct themselves will be helpful, particularly where bad news is about to be given. These may include:

- How and when opportunities for questions and comments will occur.
- Although it is to be expected that emotions will run high, verbal or physical abuse will not be tolerated.
- Although comments and opinions are welcomed, no-one will be allowed to dominate 'air time' to the exclusion of others.

STEP 2: SETTING THE SCENE AND SHARING THE MESSAGE

Objectives for Step 2
- To settle people into the Day.
- To stimulate involvement through inclusion.

The sponsor or nominated member of the top team addresses the Conference. The objective of Step 2 is to connect people to the Day by setting out the background to the Conference. The best way to do this is to talk *with* people rather than *at* them.

Unfortunately when bad news is on the agenda the temptation is for the speaker to mentally detach themselves from the audience and just impart their message in a tone that can appear distant and almost disinterested. Whether this happens because of a feeling of discomfort on the part of the speaker or a genuine disengagement from the audience is hard to tell, but the end result is the same: people will resent being talked at.

Of course good news is much easier to give (and receive): but whatever the message, the speaker must make the whole audience feel that this message is for each and every one of them. The aim is to encourage a collective feeling that 'we're all in this together'.

The process, manner and tone of this Step will depend on the reason for the Day being held, as in the examples below.

Sales Conference   You might kick off a lively, sales-oriented Day with a brisk 'scene setting' session. An example would be a discussion of market conditions in the industry sector and the current state of the competition (with the inference often being that we are doing better than they are!).

Announcing a company relocation   A more sombre note (such as announcing a relocation and accompanying reduction in headcount) will usually be introduced by the most senior person available. They will also explain the business reasons for the decisions and the support that will be in place, both for those who will be leaving and for those who will 'survive the cuts'.

The key message for the Day should be given as early as possible to stop people falsely anticipating what may be coming and to get the facts out into the open.

STEP 3: COMMENTS AND QUESTIONS FROM THE FLOOR

Objectives for Step 3
- To allow people to have their say.
- To enable the top team to hear immediate reactions to the news.

The facilitator invites comments and questions from the floor about the message that has just been given. There is an *Ask the Panel* exercise that works well at this stage, particularly where people wish to remain anonymous (see Chapter 9 for details of how to run this exercise).

There needs to be a panel, made up from members of the top team, available to answer questions and these should be addressed as honestly as possible. People will be enthused or concerned at this point, depending on the message, and are going to have questions that they need answered.

If the answers are not immediately to hand then say so. Don't make promises that can't be kept – because if they are broken later on, trust will be broken too.

STEP 4: MEMBERS OF THE TOP TEAM DEFINE AND EXPLAIN WHAT THEY SEE AS THE NEXT STEPS

Objectives for Step 4
- To keep people informed.
- To minimise ambiguity.
- To trust people with information.

Information is the key to keeping the trust and loyalty of staff at this stage. Reactions will range from depressed, fearful and possibly bitter to enthusiastic, motivated and fizzing with ideas, depending on the news that has been shared. People will tend to focus on what the news means for them personally and this Step is an opportunity for the most senior people present to try to dispel any remaining ambiguity by outlining what they see as the next steps in the process. Examples are:

- Regrouping following a harsh trading period.
- Restructuring after a round of redundancies has been completed.
- Planning to meet new business challenges and higher targets.

After the event the top team needs to continue to communicate regularly with staff to assuage any concern and anxiety about the implementation plans. They also need to publicise how staff can keep up-to-date with what's going on.

STEP 5: CONFIRM FOLLOW-UP AND CLOSE OF CONFERENCE

Objectives for Step 5
- To confirm what will happen next. This may involve written communication or further opportunities for face-to-face gatherings.
- To thank people for attending and to reiterate the key message of the Conference.
- To end the Conference on a positive note.

The sponsor ends the Conference by thanking people for their attendance and restating the key message, which should feature:

- A stirring 'call to arms' to rally people in the face of adversity.

Copies of evaluation questionnaires should be distributed in time for people to complete and hand them in as they leave the event. See Part Four for more details about evaluation, and Appendices J–N for a range of evaluation templates.

Follow-up
If further communication has been promised, ensure that it happens so that people are regularly updated.

... and finally

The Conference Day is a wonderful opportunity to keep the team abreast of developments that have a direct impact on their careers. With the main grumble amongst staff being the lack of communication they receive from their top team, why not reap the rewards of doing it well? Even if the messages you have to give are difficult for people to accept, by remaining accessible and visible you will win respect for your courage and honesty.

RECOMMENDED ROOM LAYOUT

See Appendix B for a diagram of the Conference style room layout we recommend.

13 *The Consolidation Day*

What is a Consolidation Day?

A DEFINITION

A Consolidation Day is an opportunity to confirm and fully understand where a team has arrived in terms of goals or milestones in a project or a destination point of some sort before it moves on to the next stage of its work.

It is important for a team to reflect on its efforts; what went well, what didn't, what still needs to be done and, crucially, how future work can be improved. By looking at lessons learned and identifying critical improvements, the team can come away from a Day like this with a masterplan for consolidating what is good and revising where necessary.

It is also a chance to offer praise and reassurance as well as congratulations for people's dedication, effort and ingenuity.

When to use a Consolidation Day

- When many parts of the jigsaw have been put in place and everyone needs to recognise that effort.
- To confirm the current position.
- To keep everyone on track and motivated.
- To check on what has been completed and what has been overlooked.
- To put all the pieces of the plan together for the next phase.
- To ensure a common understanding of the objectives for the next step.
- To prevent previous mistakes being repeated and improve the process.
- To review the effectiveness of previous improvements.

Key question: What is this really about?

To remain effective, teams need to understand where they are heading and where they are now. In a fast developing business environment where major changes such as restructuring are common this is especially important. A Consolidation Day is needed when the team seems disjointed and the big picture has become blurred.

A team may be working on a large project whilst all around them the organisation is in a state of flux. There are often powerful messages being created at the top of an organisation and less understanding of what these conceptual vision statements and top strategies actually mean amongst staff. A Consolidation Day can help groups understand the true meaning of strategies and concepts such as 'innovation' or 'customer focus strategies'. It consolidates understanding and encourages team members to adapt to a new direction.

 SHARK ALERT! POTENTIAL PITFALLS

- As a Consolidation Day is largely about reflection, this may frustrate those participants who are very active in their thinking style (like to get on with it). Not everyone is good at, or even comfortable with, reflecting and reviewing. If you allow the day to include consultation and group reflection as well as information input, action planning and identification of support needs, you should be able to achieve a good balance of activities to suit everyone.
- There may be resistance to attending a Consolidation Day from those who regard reflection as time wasted. It is therefore essential that you publicise the Day with stated benefits for all.
- There is a danger of being too negative about what has gone wrong in the past. This will de-motivate the team and lower the day's energy.
- Sometimes there is a danger of just 'telling' people what is going on and what to do, without ever listening to their views.

Desired outcomes: What's happened as a result of the Day?

- People are enthusiastic and clear about what they are doing.
- The team feel listened to and praised for what has gone well so far.
- The team have had time to reflect.
- Team members communicate appropriately with the rest of the organisation about intention and progress.
- The team have developed skills in reviewing and are using them regularly to good effect
- People have clarity about their role in the future.
- People can see the career possibilities they have for themselves, and the business opportunities open to the organisation.
- People communicate effectively with each other about project and career plans.
- Team members consult each other about the best ways of doing things and give each other feedback and mutual support as a result of encouragement on the Day.

How? The approach

Step 1	Welcome and introductions. Background to the Day. Agreeing ground rules.
Step 2	Identify achievements to date on the project under discussion.
Step 3	Identify what has not gone so well and what the team needs to learn to do better.
Step 4	Identify what will happen next. Give the team the opportunity to go over the plan to identify any further enhancements.
Step 5	Identify what support and resources are required to propel the team through the next phases of work.
Step 6	Agree on recommendations for action. Plan next steps and follow-up activity.

Broad outline for the Day

STEP 1: WELCOME AND INTRODUCTIONS

Objectives for Step 1
- To set peoples' expectations for the day.
- To set up an atmosphere of sharing information, ideas and solutions.
- To set up an understanding of shared responsibilities.
- To get agreement on ground rules and outcomes.

The team leader welcomes participants and introduces the Day, giving clear information about the purpose and process of the event. Remember it is a time for reflecting and catching up with what's been going on, not a time for navel gazing, so be structured about how you run the Day and emphasise the business value of reviewing and assessing progress.

The facilitator introduces the day's programme in more detail. Everyone should have received a broad outline programme with start and finish times a week or so before the event. This is especially important with a Consolidation Day because you want to manage apathy and ensure that people play their part.

State the expectations and desired outcomes from each part of the programme and gain agreement on ground rules (see Chapter 4 for examples). A particular ground rule for this event could be 'No arguing or resentment to be expressed about what *should have* or *could have* happened differently'.

If participants are not that well known to each other, introduce an icebreaker exercise designed to help them get to know each other better. Make sure you mix the groups up to enhance the effect of the exercise. Try *Mad Money* (see Chapter 9 for details of how to run this activity).

STEP 2: IDENTIFICATION ACHIEVEMENTS TO DATE

Objectives for Step 2
- To stimulate involvement through inclusion.
- To boost morale and be affirmative.
- To reflect on achievements to date.

Give the team some categories to help them reflect upon their achievements on the project. Divide the team into groups of four to six. You decide whether they would get the most out of this process by being in cross-functional groups or not.

Reflecting on our achievements: the categories
- People
- Processes
- Outcomes
- Performance
- Purpose

Add any of your own categories as appropriate. The question to ask against each category might be 'How have we done with regard to ...?'

An example of identified achievement in the People category might be: All team members studied project management skills or tools within the first two weeks of the project.

If there are less than ten participants you might want to keep the team as one and ask them to brainstorm each category.

If a group gets stuck, put the issue causing the problem up on a sheet, titled 'outstanding issues', to be dealt with later or in another way.

An effective way of summarising all the stated achievements is to ask participants to select their top one from each category and then see if there is a pattern or consensus. There doesn't have to be one, as everyone can and often does have a different perspective on success but it may be interesting or significant.

STEP 3: IDENTIFICATION OF WHAT HAS NOT GONE SO WELL

Objectives for Step 3
- To make the things that haven't gone so well evident to everyone in the team.
- To promote reflection.
- To help the team identify and face up to the negative issues it needs to address.
- To identify best practice and tried and tested improvement techniques.
- To identify what may have been missed or overlooked.
- To identify what the team needs to learn to do better.

A recommended process here is to use the same categories as in Step 2, keep the same groups and ask them to identify what didn't go so well to date. The groups then need to work out what the lessons are as a result of their findings. The facilitator asks the groups to present their findings back to the main group including their recommendations for improvement and learning.

STEP 4: IDENTIFY WHAT WILL HAPPEN NEXT

Objectives for Step 4
- To ensure that everyone has a common understanding about what is expected of them during the next phase of work.
- To identify improvements and flesh them out into practical solutions.
- To ensure that all aspects of future work have been considered.

A good place to start is for the sponsor or leader to give a presentation of what is to happen next on the project or in the strategy and how it will be implemented. Then the facilitator can open this up for discussion either in groups or as a whole group. You are seeking to glean three pieces of feedback from the discussion:

- What are immediate reactions?
- Is there anything missing?
- Does anything need to be adjusted?

Capture the views for the team leader to take back to work for consideration.

STEP 5: IDENTIFY WHAT SUPPORT AND RESOURCES ARE REQUIRED

Objectives for Step 5
- To ensure that the team has thought of everything that it will need to complete the next phase successfully.
- To be realistic about the opportunities and constraints of working within the organisation.
- To identify the support and resources needed.

The facilitator or leader will stimulate the team's thinking by asking the following types of questions:

- What support is needed to help the team to the next stage or milestone of achievement?
- What resources are needed?
- What communication must take place to inform the rest of the organisation of the team's activities?
- What political sensitivities and PR need to be considered (for example, in order to gain sponsorship the team needs to ensure that the project is publicised skilfully)?
- What opportunities still exist for the team to exploit?
- What constraints could potentially foil its attempts to be successful?

Give the groups 20 minutes to discuss the above questions and prepare mini-presentations to feed back their thoughts to the team. Invite discussion after each presentation for up to 10 minutes only; this will ensure that everyone feels consulted and that you will have heard most views and ideas.

The result will be a list of requirements, some ideas for new opportunities and possibly a list of potential problems to overcome.

STEP 6: AGREE ON RECOMMENDATIONS FOR ACTION. PLAN NEXT STEPS AND FOLLOW-UP ACTIVITY

Objectives for Step 6
- To create a plan of action from the results of Step 5.
- To gain agreement from everyone on what will improve performance and processes.
- To ensure that everyone has had an opportunity to express a view and exercise their choice on whether to commit to the next phase or not.
- To check that each action plan has an owner and an agreed time for its completion.

The groups need to prioritise the lists based on defined criteria (for example *must do/would like to do, urgent/important* or a set of criteria of your own choosing). Alternatively the technique *Ranking and Rating* shown at Appendix G might be helpful.

The key objective for Step 6 is to arrive at a prioritised list of actions based on the team's recommendations. The facilitator will help the team to draw up action plans encompassing the following information:

- Who is responsible?
- What actions will they take?

- When will they do it by?
- Who will they do it with?
- Who else needs to know?

The people named are now deemed responsible in the eyes of the team for implementing the team action plans.

Team members are now invited to declare whether or not they are prepared to commit to the next phase of work. In order to get as many views as possible consider using the following techniques:

1 Anonymous voting through a ballot box;
2 Focused group discussions, ending in each group stating whether there is unanimous agreement or mixed opinion; or
3 Question and answer session where questions are anonymously put in a hat and answered by a panel made up of the sponsor(s) and any other advisors. The great benefits of this exercise are many-fold. It gives qualitative and quantitative feedback regarding the level of commitment; opportunities to address resistance and concerns; and realigns misconceptions where they occur.

If you discover that a large majority of people have chosen to try and opt out of committing to the next phase, we recommend that you prepare and plan to start again and design a programme of persuasion unless you are prepared to enforce the issue (see Chapter 11, the Challenge of Change Day). Where only a minority have expressed dissent, invite them to one-to-one discussions with you to explore their thoughts further.

Communicate to the team how you intend to monitor and review progress.

Remember to request evaluation using your selected evaluation questionnaire. See Appendices J–N for a choice of templates and Part Four for more information.

… and finally

Consolidation is good practice. It is the critical first stage in forecasting the future. It also helps people cope with and (in some cases) thrive on perpetual change as they will be able to see and hopefully understand why the change is happening. The consolidation process enables teams to identify, in good time, what skills and processes they will need to successfully deal with their projects and other work.

This event provides a necessary safety net, preventing deadline slippage, resource wastage and a skills gap when you can least afford it. It also gives you a chance to pre-empt any demoralisation. This type of event gives you as a team leader a really good feel for how every aspect of the work is going and importantly how the team feels about it and each other.

RECOMMENDED ROOM LAYOUT

Choose a layout where the team feels comfortable and where they can be easily consulted. A formal layout may create barriers. See Appendix B for layout choices.

14 *The Consultation Day*

What is a Consultation Day?

A DEFINITION

The Consultation Day offers teams the chance to confer about issues that will affect them all by inviting them to discuss and debate agreed topics.

The agenda for the Consultation Day is usually set by team leaders and managers who will restrict the scope of the consultation in that they will be consulting on *how* something is to be achieved rather than *what* or *why*.

A Consultation Day may be a boisterous, dynamic affair. If it has been a long time since people's views have been sought or if the discussion topics are close to the hearts of the group, expect to hear some lively exchanges. This is a healthy sign that people are engaging with the questions and are prepared to share their thoughts.

At an early stage in the Day people must be made aware of all the opportunities and constraints impacting on the issues. This will make clear how far they can go with creative thought and where the restrictions lie. The constraints should be genuine and relevant. Excuses will swiftly be recognised for what they are!

A Consultation Day builds goodwill. To prevent it ebbing away after the event, team leaders have a responsibility to give serious consideration to ideas raised and timely feedback to participants on the decided outcomes.

When to use a Consultation Day

- Where you need to implement a new business process and want to source the best possible method of implementation.
- Where you are considering the implementation of a new business process and want to consult on pro's and con's.
- When it is time to consult the team and draw on their practical knowledge. What can you learn from their past experiences that will benefit the team in the future? People might have excellent ideas on how to proceed: ensure that they are heard.
- To ensure that everyone's ideas are heard: so good ideas won't slip through the net.
- When you want or need to hear people's opinions.
- When you've been told to consult with the team: many people are aware of the impact of false consultation. Make sure yours is genuine and not merely a process whereby you ignore their ideas after the event.

- When you want to keep people happy: consultation promotes involvement and commitment.
- When complying with the law and Human Resource practices, for example on statutory consultation prior to redundancies.
- When collecting data, ideas, views or opinions prior to making a decision.
- When you genuinely want people to help you make a decision as part of the process (see Chapter 16, The Decision Making Day).

Key Question: What is this really about?

The Consultation Day is all about team leaders demonstrating real inclusion and genuinely gathering knowledge and judgement to strengthen decision making. Nobody can have all the answers and by signalling willingness to hear what people know and considering acting on their ideas, managers are taking an important step towards encouraging stronger group identity and team spirit that can be capitalised upon when times get hard.

Consultation is an adult process, best characterised by a highly participative style. If leaders invite people's views they must expect to hear frank and forthright comments as a result and this is to be welcomed. Provided that these comments remain constructive they will promote animated, healthy debate however if comments degenerate into grumbling or accusation, battle lines may be drawn! See Chapter 7, Handling different event roles, for guidance on appropriate roles and facilitation techniques.

 SHARK ALERT! POTENTIAL PITFALLS

- Be selective: there are some decisions you won't want to consult groups on, for example, strategy for more junior groups or pay and bonuses for more senior staff.
- Be aware of the difference between *real* and *faux* consultation. The first establishes people's thoughts and opinions – the second does the same but then completely ignores them.
- Setting accurate expectations is key to the success of a Consultation Day. People need to understand that although their thoughts are being welcomed, no promises are being made to them about what actions will be taken as a result of the consultation. Neglecting to state this may result in unrealistic hopes being raised.
- Make sure that you have consulted with everyone in the team. If people are forgotten or ignored you risk creating future saboteurs to team harmony
- Be as open about the consultation as you can. Tempting though it is to lobby one or two key decision makers behind the scenes, if word gets about that you have already taken the decision and are merely paying 'lip service' to the consultation then your Day will collapse like a flat soufflé.
- Flexibility is an essential attribute for team leaders running a Consultation Day. To slavishly pursue an idea when better, more practical ones have been proposed will undermine your leadership and appear uncaring.

Desired outcomes: What's happened as a result of the Day?

- People are willing to speak their mind about issues impacting on them as individuals or team members.

- Team members do not take it personally if ideas are rejected as impractical or if the time is not right to proceed. Instead they will be positive and eager to look for new ideas to propose.
- People feel that they matter.
- The team constructively discusses matters of importance to them.
- Lines of communication between the team and the leader are open.
- Ideas are freely exchanged between team members and between the leader and the team.
- Great ideas have been proposed and accepted.
- People trust their colleagues and the team leader to treat their views with respect.

How? The approach

Step 1   Welcome and introductions. Understanding the background to the Day. Reviewing objectives and agreeing ground rules.
Step 2   Generating ideas – starting to focus on the main consultation topic for the Day.
Step 3   Gathering and classifying data.
Step 4   Evaluating classified ideas.
Step 5   Agree on recommended actions, next steps and follow-up.

Broad outline for the Day

STEP 1: WELCOME AND INTRODUCTIONS

Objectives for Step 1
- To encourage confidence that the team leadership really values people's opinions.
- To foster an atmosphere of trust and openness in the room.
- To set expectations for the rest of the Day.

The sponsor welcomes participants and introduces the Day. By running a Consultation Day, the organisation is explicitly demonstrating its desire to understand a particular problem or situation from the perspective of its staff. Clearly communicating this desire at the beginning of the Day will start the event off on an encouraging note and send out the right signals to the team, i.e. that the leadership wants to hear their thoughts on issues of importance. An attention-grabbing introduction that sells the benefits of the Day will keep people alert and interested in what is to follow.

As part of Step 1 expectations need to be set by the team leader or sponsor. This will include agreement on what can realistically be covered at the event. The facilitator leads the agreement of ground rules for the Day (see Chapter 4). A key ground rule for the Consultation Day could be:

- All ideas will be considered but not all ideas will be adopted.

Outline the objectives for the Day. Consultation with the team should start as early as possible as lengthy preambles can bore people. Similarly, you may wish to avoid long-winded introductory exercises and instead go for a quick icebreaker (such as *Hopes for the Day*) to liven the team up. See Chapter 9 for this and other example icebreakers.

As you would expect, a Consultation Day will focus on gathering data on one or more issues. We encourage you to prominently feature small team work on this Day. An ideal small group number is no more than eight.

STEP 2: GENERATING IDEAS

Objectives for Step 2
- To facilitate energetic discussion.
- To manage differences of opinion so that people can still work together productively.
- To generate ideas.

Divide people into small groups (you determine the criteria for the mix). We suggest a brainstorming exercise. See Appendix E for the brainstorming process.

Starting with a theme or a question that requires a response, generate lots of different ideas and capture them on a flipchart ready for Step 3.

STEP 3: GATHERING AND CLASSIFYING DATA

Objectives for Step 3
- To arrange the data into a format that enables evaluation for the best ideas
- To allow for generation of questions and thoughts to check understanding

Step 3 is an interim Step which illuminates patterns, priorities and perspectives emerging from the wealth of data collected. There is an opportunity to check understanding of each others' ideas. At this stage concepts of logic and context are being introduced because you have to start narrowing down your choices. It is usually impossible to implement every single idea generated; resources would not stretch that far!

Classifying techniques   Here are a variety of classifying techniques for you to choose from:
- Chronological order: when brainstorming a range of tasks that may need to be carried out you will be able to organise them according to time priority.
- Connections: an easy visual representation where items that can be classified together are connected up or linked.
- Picking a winner: ask people to select their top three choices from the range available to them from all the lists. The facilitator then checks for and identifies any commonality, divergence and themes.

Remember to allow people to check their understanding of the ideas.

STEP 4: EVALUATING CLASSIFIED IDEAS

Objectives for Step 4
- To select the most fitting ideas to suit current circumstances.
- To introduce a note of practicality into the proceedings.
- To translate the selected ideas into an action plan.

Having combined themes, eliminated duplicates and put similar ideas together in a coherent way, ask the team to vote again: this time selecting their top 'one and only' choice.

The team exercise *Flipping the Coin* will help in the evaluation of the remaining ideas. This exercise uses the top choices that you asked people to make at Step 3. It reveals the advantages and disadvantages of their choice that may not have been immediately apparent. See Chapter 9 for detailed instructions of how to run this exercise.

STEP 5: AGREE ON RECOMMENDED ACTIONS, NEXT STEPS AND FOLLOW-UP

Objectives for Step 5

You now have a list of issues that have been quality-assessed (pro's and con's). Eliminate those that have no obvious advantages. The team leader takes away the rest of the list for further investigation if required. The consultation process is over. If you would like the group to make a decision based on the best ideas, refer to the Decision Making Day (Chapter 16).

We recommend that you ask participants to evaluate their experience of the Day. See Part Four for more detail on evaluation, and Appendices J–N for sample evaluation sheets.

Thank everybody, inform them what you are going to do and when they can expect further news.

… and finally

The Consultation Day offers team leaders a unique opportunity to really 'connect' with their people; to hear their voice and be seen to be listening. Having invested in your team and gained their insight and expertise, you are now likely to have goodwill, enthusiasm and qualitative material on which to base decisions.

RECOMMENDED ROOM LAYOUT

For groups of up to 20 participants we recommend Cabaret style seating. For larger groups, go for Theatre style plus syndicate rooms to suit the numbers. See Appendix B for choice of room layouts.

15 *The Creativity Day*

What is a Creativity Day?

A DEFINITION

A Creativity Day is an opportunity for an outpouring of innovative ideas in response to a new set of challenges, constraints and opportunities.

A lively and upbeat Legendary Away Day, the Creativity Day offers teams a chance to explore previously uncharted creative waters in order to identify original ways of meeting their existing or new objectives.

In order to provide a sharp focus for the Day, there should be a primary objective or challenge for the group to meet. People need to understand and accept the necessity of moving away from the past and looking at new methods and new ways of thinking that will be of benefit in the future. Changing business demands may require real and continuous innovation and the Creativity Day gives the team a blank sheet on which to sketch its blueprint for future success. At the same time, it provides a structured approach towards generating ideas, identifying those most likely to succeed and planning the first steps towards implementation.

When to use a Creativity Day

- When people are no longer enthused by using existing methods of working and the team needs to have a creative rethink.
- When existing methods are no longer working effectively.
- When a new challenge or problem exists that demands an inspired solution.
- Where there is insufficient time to follow the tried and tested ways of working, yet a safe solution is still required, for example when deadlines have brought forward due to external constraints but a quality result is still required.
- To draw upon the creative power of the whole team to be inclusive and to gather more creative material.
- When the right conditions exist within the team to allow for a mutually supportive brainstorming session, where everyone's views will be considered and nothing is dismissed out of hand.
- Creative thinking is a set of skills (such as being structured, allowing inspiration and evaluating) and also a useful teambuilding activity.

Key question: What is this really about?

To remain effective, teams need to keep developing. Models of success keep changing, as do client requirements, and this Day is about ensuring that a team does not rest on its laurels by constantly recreating past successes and neglecting the key creative skills and attributes that made it successful in the first place. This process of continuous growth and meeting the challenges of the future means constantly encouraging people to contribute their suggestions and then ensuring that those suggestions are listened to. Encouraging teams to be creative together often results in them sharing their original ideas, allowing each other to develop the concepts into workable solutions.

SHARK ALERT! POTENTIAL PITFALLS

- Keep a watchful eye on your budget. It is easy to let spending spiral out of control when trying to introduce new systems.
- It is possible to waste not only finance but also time and effort (for example through unnecessary duplication of tasks – how many people need to check the arrangements and how often?).
- Don't pursue creativity just to shake everybody up unless you have a key business purpose for doing so.
- Not everyone wants to voice new ideas, particularly if they are afraid of looking foolish (either on a personal or a professional level). The creation of a safe, supportive environment will minimise this risk.
- Check that the desire for innovation is not being driven by professional rivalry or personal vanity (yours or someone else's).
- Ensure that the lessons of the past are not swept aside if they can be useful for future development.
- Watch out for examples of unsupportive behaviour during the session and if you see them, be ready to step in and draw the attention of the group to the agreed ground rules which should include 'supportive behaviour from each participant'.
- Before rushing to adopt recommended solutions from the Creativity Day, check as far as possible to make sure that they are practical; the disappointment of finding at a later date that a idea has to be shelved for lack of practicality will generate resentment and a lack of support for future Creativity Days.
- The team may not come up with a suitable solution on the day. They should be encouraged to think of a solution but not bullied to do so. Another Creativity event may be needed which looks at the issues from a different perspective.

Desired outcomes: What's happened as a result of the Day?

- People are enthused: there is a 'buzz' around the place.
- They have had fun.
- They feel as though they have been heard.
- They are looking to the future.
- They have shown respect to their colleagues.
- The team is ready to meet new challenges.
- People are more productive at work.

- The team demonstrates positive thoughts and behaviour.
- People are more open to new working processes.
- People think more laterally.

How? The approach

Step 1   Welcome and introductions. Background to the event. Reviewing objectives and agreeing ground rules.
Step 2   Generating creativity.
Step 3   Focus on creative ways of meeting the main objective.
Step 4   Agree on recommended actions.
Step 5   Next steps and follow-up.

Broad outline for the Day

STEP 1: WELCOME AND INTRODUCTIONS

Objectives for Step 1
- To build people's confidence in one another and the facilitator.
- To set up an atmosphere that encourages the sharing of ideas.
- To create a heightened sense of anticipation.
- To generate energy.
- To emphasise that it is OK to propose radical solutions: to 'fly without a safety net'. Nothing will be discounted at this early stage.

The sponsor welcomes participants and introduces the Away Day, giving brief but incisive comment about the event. Holding a Creativity Day implies a need (or a desire) to look at things differently and the introduction is the place to outline the main driving forces behind the change. It is a time for energising people: not for threatening them with gloomy prophecies about what will happen if the change doesn't take place!

The facilitator leads the setting of ground rules and seeks agreement from the group (see Chapter 4). Key ground rules for the Creativity Day might include:

- Each participant to demonstrate supportive behaviour to the rest of the group.
- Everyone to be equally supportive of expected *and* unexpected ideas.
- Keep an open mind. From an idea that sounds daft at first may emerge the basis of a phenomenal solution.

Outline the primary (and secondary) objectives for the Day. With a Creativity Day, at least some measure of consultation with the group is essential and as huge numbers of participants will be unusual on a Day such as this (usually 20 maximum), you may wish to begin this process as early as possible by inviting input into decisions about:

- What is practical to achieve in the available time.
- What else can be achieved if the main objective is completed quickly (for example any secondary objectives).

Introductory exercise It is highly recommended that people start talking to each other as soon as possible as this eases the way into working together on tasks. The best starting point is to use an exercise to help this process. The selected icebreaker should be fairly brief and certainly light-hearted in tone (how light-hearted depends on how comfortable people are with one another). We suggest that you consider *Getting to know you* or if you have a very outgoing group who know each other well try *Crocodiles*. See Chapter 9 for full details of how to run these exercises.

STEP 2: GENERATING CREATIVITY

Objectives for Step 2
- To introduce a blast of energy into the Day.
- To develop trust between the group so that they become less inhibited about suggesting 'off the wall' ideas.

The idea of Step 2 is not instantly to come up with a solution that meets the objective of the Day, but to introduce some energy and vitality into the event. A valuable tool to help you would be a fast-paced 'brainstorming' session. Brainstorming sessions have their own rules (see Appendix E) and to get the best value from this session it is advisable for the facilitator to suggest additional ground rules for the brainstorm. These should include:

- Welcome 'offbeat' ideas.
- No ideas discounted.
- No-one to criticise the ideas of others at this stage: not even constructively.
- Encourage lateral thinking.
- Embrace unexpected ideas.

There are a range of techniques such as time-lining, brainstorming, lateral thinking exercises, visual stimulation and association (see Appendix F for *our* range of Creativity Tools).

STEP 3: FOCUS ON CREATIVE WAYS OF MEETING THE MAIN OBJECTIVE

Objectives for Step 3
- To identify the most popular options.
- To narrow down the list of options to a maximum of three.
- To introduce a note of practicality without dampening enthusiasm.

This is the point at which the facilitator needs to introduce a further element of rationality into the proceedings, without stifling the fervour that has been generated. We see this as a three-stage process:

1 To decide which are the *most popular* options amongst the group.
2 For people to think about and discuss the *practicalities* of each option.
3 To give the group the opportunity of raising and addressing any serious doubts or questions they may have.

Some Days are designed just for the generation of creative ideas. Other Days may include the generation of ideas and the setting up of sub-groups to work together after the event to develop the ideas further towards implementation.

At this third step, it is crucial that everyone who has something to say about the practicality of the suggested options gets their chance. Keep an open mind about the comments being made and try to keep your own views out of the equation. All voices in the room should be encouraged to contribute, from the most vocal (although it may or may not be true that 'empty vessels make the loudest noise') to the quietest in the group. Part of the facilitator's role is to achieve a balance between allowing the loudest in the group to be fully heard whilst diplomatically preventing them from dominating proceedings and stopping others from airing their views. Here is the process: your facilitator will guide you stage-by-stage.

Narrowing the field: the popularity contest

As your team reaches the decision-making stages of the process, it is vital that more forceful personalities don't try to use the relaxed and trusting atmosphere that has been built up to bully others and impose their personal choices on them. Everyone's selections should be made on the basis of free choice.

There are many ways of setting up this process. We think the most straightforward is a voting system or you could use a more thorough technique such as *Ranking and Rating* as outlined in Appendix G. Take note that no perceived advantages and disadvantages are attached to suggestions at this stage as the group will have a chance to debate these later.

Three preferred options should emerge from the *popularity contest* to take forward to meet the *logistical challenge.*

The logistical challenge

Once the facilitator has summarised the voting and assessed which options have attracted most votes, the next stage asks the group to begin assessing the relative 'pluses' and 'minuses' of trying to introduce each option, according to their personal views. This is where perceived advantages and disadvantages of each option can be debated. To focus thinking, divide the group into syndicate teams (maximum six per group) and ask them to think about the following questions in relation to each of the top three options:

- How practical is the option as it currently stands?
- What adjustments would have to be made if this option were to be implemented?
- What would be the knock-on effect on others (individuals and teams) if this option was to be implemented?
- Whose support would we need to win in order to ensure successful implementation?
- How long would we need to allow for the lobbying process?
- How long do we estimate would be needed for the implementation process?
- How long do we have available for the implementation process?
- Do we have any immediately identifiable champions for the idea?
- What are the estimated design/implementation costs?
- What is our budget for design and implementation?
- What value does this option add to our existing processes?
- What new value does it add which may not be immediately apparent?
- What options for further development or new business processes spring out of this idea?

At the end of the activity, each syndicate group will be asked to report back to the main group with the information on their preferred option.

Questions and concerns   There are likely to be a number of questions and concerns raised at this third stage and it is important that they are heard and addressed to the satisfaction of the questioner. Otherwise there is a risk that their concerns may come back to haunt the team later on, prompting accusations of 'I told you so'.

Handle any dissent that threatens to damage the carefully-nurtured team dynamic with courtesy but firmness to prevent the group from stumbling into grumbling mode.

Any questions or concerns that are not satisfactorily resolved, or that need to be referred to others within the group, should be saved and fed back to the plenary group to ensure completeness and so that discussion does not become too fragmented.

STEP 4: AGREE ON RECOMMENDED ACTIONS

Objectives for Step 4
- To gain team commitment to a recommendation to be taken forward.
- To check that there is no remaining serious dissent among the group.
- Capture the outstanding ideas in an 'ideas bank' for possible future use as they may better suit a different set of circumstances or may prove, in reality, to be the most practical.
- Agree who should hold the 'ideas bank', how and when it should be accessed.

This is where broad consensus needs to be achieved on which recommendation (if any) will be adopted for further exploration.

Step 4 should be carried out in plenary session, with the whole group working together.

Hopefully there will be general agreement as to a preferred option. However there may be some degree of tweaking or calibration needed to address any final questions or concerns before the recommendation is accepted by the group.

You need to gain agreement that the whole team will own the solution so that no one person is credited or blamed for success or failure. This is a team effort!

The next step is for the facilitator or team leader to propose one option to the group in its final (adjusted) format and to invite the group's acceptance of the recommendation to go forward to Step 5.

STEP 5: NEXT STEPS AND FOLLOW-UP

Objectives for Step 5
- To gain agreement for the next steps in the process.
- To agree how the rest of the team will be kept informed of progress.

Gaining acceptance of one recommended option sometimes looks like the easy part of the challenge compared to agreeing the next steps and follow-up. After all, researching the feasibility of introducing a pioneering concept can be a daunting prospect, not to say time-consuming. For this reason many team members will stay quiet rather than volunteer for extra work, in the hope that this onerous task will fall to someone else. This stage is the last in the Day and for this reason people may be feeling tired. An energising activity just before you enter 'the final lap' is a good idea (we recommend *Time for Tea* see Chapter 9).

Follow-up

Develop a simple action plan for the group to set out who will do what, and by when. The team leader will be responsible for the fair allocation of the tasks to the team. There may be some obvious candidates for certain of the tasks and these should be allocated first. In many cases volunteers will come forward, however if they don't, it will be the responsibility of the team leader to allocate tasks on a reasonable basis. Who is most suited? Is their current workload heavy or light? Don't be tempted to pick the 'willing workhorses' all the time!

Remember to evaluate. Ask your team what they thought of the Day as well as requesting more detailed evaluation. See Appendices J–N for a range of evaluation questionnaires and Part Four for more information on the benefits of evaluation.

The team leader should also monitor progress. The team will expect to be regularly updated. A major advantage of a Day such as this is that the team feels a strong sense of ownership for the resulting plan: keep them informed and involved throughout the whole process.

… and finally

The Creativity Day is an inspiring opportunity not only to get the whole team working together, but also to give its imagination free rein. Now is the time to harness creativity to realism and lead your team on to future success.

RECOMMENDED ROOM LAYOUT

The room layout will depend on what activities you are planning to do, for example, if you want people to build anything then they need either floor space or table space on which to do it.

People like room to think. We recommend that you go for the largest space you can afford or source. Otherwise go for syndicate rooms (how many will depend on numbers) for your small groups to work in. Try not to create formality in your room set-up if you want people to think freely. See Appendix B for a choice of room layouts.

16 *The Decision Making Day*

What is a Decision Making Day?

A DEFINITION

Although it is dazzlingly obvious that the Decision Making Day is designed to help a group arrive at a decision, more challenging questions to ask are '*how* does your group make a decision' and '*why* would it want to?' This chapter gives you explicit guidance on how to design and run an event which results in sound team decisions being formulated. If you follow our route plan you will discover the *how* and the *why* in detail which you can transfer to your own circumstances.

When to use a Decision Making Day

- When you need to cut through conflict due to opposing positions and arguments about an issue.
- When you want the best decision possible.
- When you need to choose from a range of options and solutions.
- When you want an inexperienced team to learn how to make decisions together.
- When you want a team to take responsibility and decision making can be the process by which this is achieved.
- Where you want the team's range of experiences and skills to be employed usefully in finalising a decision.
- When a senior management team needs to take a difficult decision.
- When you want lateral and creative thought to have gone into the process of decision making.

Key question: What is this really about?

Different people hold different views about the issues they face. Unless they come together and find a way to compromise or dovetail their positions, there is no way forward. How many groups of people do you know who seem to prefer arguing to action or who eventually get so utterly fed up with the inertia and stalling which surrounds them that they eventually take action and demand resolution? This will not happen to your team if you have opted for determined action and the use of techniques by selecting this Day.

 ## SHARK ALERT! POTENTIAL PITFALLS

- The wrong people are at the event. They could be ill-informed, unable or unwilling to take responsibility. They may not have power vested in them to take decisions.
- Consider who is sponsoring and facilitating the event. They need to be encouraging with a participative style; they also need to have a strong grip on the process and a firm control of the group's behaviour.
- There are no processes in place to help the group reach a decision. They may instead flounder about without purpose, wasting time and effort.
- The group or manager may try to duck out of taking responsibility for action points, leaving everyone frustrated: and the facilitator might let them get away with it.
- Certain members of the team are more dominant than others and may try to seize control of the process or the final decision. Only a strong facilitator will block them and create a more appropriate process.
- Sometimes the difficulty of the decision-making process results in a slow pace being followed and frustration setting in. This can cause people to withdraw.
- People may not understand each other's thinking; either because they don't want to, or they genuinely don't understand.
- More junior members of staff may not have previously experienced being involved in a consultative decision-making process and may not be aware of how to contribute.
- If people have a vested interest in seeing things from their point of view, they may become quite emotional and whilst this might be difficult to manage it *is* real, and some sensitivity in handling it is needed.
- The decision is over-ruled by senior managers.
- If some team members appear to have lost out by conceding a lot make sure they don't lose face
- Seniors may dominate juniors.
- Beware of false decision-making, where a leader asks the group to make a decision but doesn't like their choice.

Desired outcomes: What's happened as a result of the Day?

- There is a decision!
- People are abiding by that decision.
- People are confident that it is the right decision.
- People are still co-operative with each other.
- There are no grudges or bad feelings left over from the event.

How? The approach

Step 1   Welcome and introductions. Background to the event. Reviewing objectives and agreeing ground rules.

Step 2   Exploration – uncovering the issues.

Step 3   Debate – explaining our positions.
Step 4   Decision - cutting through any conflicts of interest and choosing.
Step 5   Check the decision and identify the implementation needs.
Step 6   Action planning and closing the Day.

Broad outline for the Day

STEP 1: WELCOME AND INTRODUCTIONS

Objectives for Step 1
- To set the scene for the Day.
- To ensure everyone introduces themselves.
- To make sure that the outcomes and objectives are clear.
- To ensure that the ground rules for the day are agreed.

The leader or facilitator introduces the Day and ensures that the familiarisation process begins early in the event. One way of doing this is to seat participants in cabaret style (see Appendix B) and ask them to introduce themselves to each other if they don't already know one another. Ask them to state their personal expectations and concerns for the Day (see Chapter 9 for an icebreaker called *Hopes for the Day* that you may wish to try).

The outcomes and objectives are explained fully along with brief details of what has driven the need for this Day. The facilitator leads the agreement of ground rules. See Chapter 4 for more information on setting, agreeing and using ground rules or look through the other Legendary Away Days. Here are some examples of ground rules that we have found work well for this particular Day.

- All are jointly responsible for the Day.
- Use all available skills and perspectives.
- Avoid blame.
- Be committed to the decision.

STEP 2: EXPLORATION – UNCOVERING THE ISSUES

Objectives for Step 2
- To understand what the recommended options are.
- To understand how the recommended options were developed.
- To understand what the recommended options mean.
- To allow for the introduction of new options if needed.

The sponsor or team leader explains what the options are and how they were arrived at. Any initial questions are handled at this stage.

The facilitator shows the group each option and discusses its meaning with them until a common understanding is reached. The facilitator also checks for agreement on each option including any new suggestions that may have arisen.

Only when there are no more outstanding questions or objections can you move on.

STEP 3: DEBATE – EXPLAINING OUR POSITIONS

Objectives for Step 3
- To enable people to offer to the group their positions, their arguments and their opinions
- To let people have their say for an agreed length of time.
- To allow people to debate the pro's and con's of each option or their preferred stance.

It is best if this part of the Day is well structured and that fairness is maintained – if one person is given 5 minutes to present their case then everyone else must be given the same amount of time.

Larger groups, smaller groups Where there are more than 10 participants, divide them into sub-groups and give them an allocated period of time to discuss and debate the options. Ask them to present back their findings. Once all the presentations are complete and the whole group's views are in the open, you have a further choice to make. Either:

- Introduce a helpful technique for selecting the final option, for example *Ranking and Rating* (see Appendix G)

or

- Mix the groups up again and ask them to make a decision within a set period of time. You may end up with the same number of chosen options as you have sub-groups. Voting would be an obvious next step although the whole group may prefer to discuss and then reach consensus through influence and negotiation.

If you have less than 10 participants, give everyone individual and equal presentation time to persuade their colleagues and then allow a further hour's debate after which they *must* make a decision.

STEP 4: DECISION – CUTTING THROUGH ANY CONFLICTS OF INTEREST AND CHOOSING

Objective for Step 4
There will need to come a time when discussion must end or else no decision will be made. It is sometimes difficult to stop people continuing the debate, particularly when their preferred options have not been favoured by the majority. Nonetheless, show your mettle as the facilitator, sponsor or team leader and put a stop to the prevarication.

A decision must be made one way or another. See Step 3 for some techniques to assist you or Appendix G for further ideas.

STEP 5: CHECK THE DECISION AND IDENTIFY THE IMPLEMENTATION NEEDS

Objectives for Step 5
- Ensure that the decision is understood.
- Identify the impact of the decision on others outside the group.

- Identify what communication needs are required to smooth the implementation process.

At Step 5 we recommend that you select the *Flipping the Coin* exercise (see Chapter 9) because it enables the team or small groups to think about the impact of this decision and its associated implications.

The results of this exercise will enable the team to identify what they need to communicate to others and in what manner.

STEP 6: ACTION PLANNING AND CLOSING THE DAY

Objectives for Step 6

- Create an action plan for implementing the decision.
- Close the Day in an appropriate manner, ensuring that there is no residual conflict.

Before you can implement the chosen decision ensure that you are working from a clear, detailed action plan which states who will do what, by when.

Close the Day by ensuring that as much residual bad feeling as possible is left behind at the event. An exercise to help you achieve this is *Revelation Cards* (see Chapter 9 for full details). This way the focus is on the future and not on the past.

All that remains is to request that participants review the Day by completing an evaluation questionnaire so that you can get an immediate sense of how the Day went and if there are any outstanding issues that you were unaware of. See Part Four and Appendices J–N for more information about evaluation and questionnaires.

... and finally

Remember to thank everyone for their participation.

RECOMMENDED ROOM LAYOUT

For 10 participants or less, go for Boardroom style plus a syndicate room. For large groups (10 to 30) opt for Cabaret style and for even larger groups (30+) Theatre style with syndicate facilities. See Appendix B for choice of room layouts.

17 *The Morale Boosting Day*

What is a Morale Boosting Day? A definition

A highly participative Day designed to reinvigorate and refocus jaded or demotivated groups.

By identifying and getting to the heart of the real issues, not just the symptoms, this event will provoke a shift in attitudes and encourage teams to go forward with a new, more positive approach to achieving their goals.

 ## SHARK ALERT!

Proceed with caution! Success in running this Day will demand a high level of sensitivity to people's feelings. It is not the role of the facilitator to deny the emotions that people are experiencing, but to provide an atmosphere in which they can think about the real issues, deal with the most urgent ones and agree a way forward.

When to use the Morale Boosting Day

When the team seems to be demotivated and there is evidence (however minor) of conflict amongst group members. Indicators of minor conflict need to be addressed at an early stage as they will escalate if left unattended.

Some or all of the following symptoms may be in evidence:

- Squabbling amongst group members.
- Some group members have left for other jobs and others are job seeking.
- A general reluctance to carry out tasks together.
- Managers are being blamed for many things.
- Cynicism is rampant.
- Some group members have withdrawn from group activities.
- Others are being excluded from the team either intentionally or incidentally.
- A blame culture is prevalent: both between managers and staff, and across peer groups.

Key question: What is this really about?

In these circumstances it is highly likely that individual and team productivity are being damaged. Morale needs to be boosted, and quickly, if longer-term crises and group implosion are to be avoided. Urgent action is needed to get the team working together productively and to raise levels of enthusiasm. Sweeping the issues under the carpet will not work; instead the real reasons for the depletion in morale need to be addressed and explored.

During the Morale Boosting Day, people will be encouraged to consider the real issues; people's feelings will be acknowledged and not sidelined. Lively, open and honest debate will be expected and encouraged, and the team will emerge reinvigorated as a result.

SHARK ALERT! POTENTIAL PITFALLS

- Individuals may have their own (overt or hidden) agendas for the day. Uncovering the real agenda and what matters to people is a vital step towards improving morale.
- A temptation may be to dismiss or ignore people's emotions and so avoid the discomfort of having to address them. This will store up problems for the future and when they recur, they can be twice as powerful!
- Teams may try to use the Day as a 'moaning session' if you don't maintain structure and control.
- If you don't allow some release of negativity, the team will feel controlled and over-managed. You will need to find the right balance.
- If you don't listen to the team's complaints and concerns, they won't want to work with you.
- Unless the Day is based on reality, for example a major restructuring is taking place throughout the organisation and most people are unhappy about it, your expectations are likely to be thwarted.

Desired outcomes: What's happened as a result of the Day?

- Morale has improved.
- Trust is in evidence and consequently people are prepared to share ideas and voice concerns.
- Individual team members are motivated about their tasks and goals.
- People feel that their managers care about them and their opinions.
- People feel that they are being recognised for their efforts and achievements.
- Team members readily network and discuss work issues with each other.
- People are looking to the future and not dwelling on past negativity.
- The team is able to identify and work towards meeting team objectives.
- There is greater purpose to the way people go about their daily work.
- There is a reduction in blaming others and an increase in self-responsibility.

How? The approach

Step 1   Welcome and introductions. Setting the scene and agreeing ground rules.

Step 2   Generating steam – a session for people to let off steam and say what is worrying or aggravating them.

Step 3   Identifying the real issues: what are the main and most pressing to address?
Step 4   What are the steps to go forward? Realistically what can be achieved today?
Step 5   Confirm team and individual attributes.
Step 6   Identify support needs (team and individual).
Step 7   Group finale – networking exercise.

Broad outline for the Day

STEP 1: WELCOME AND INTRODUCTIONS

Objectives for Step 1
- To set the scene for the Day.
- To establish a supportive tone right at the outset.
- To set expectations by explaining what the event is designed to achieve as well as what it is *not* designed for.
- To agree ground rules.
- To create an environment of trust.

The event leader or the sponsor welcomes the team and introduces the Day. The purpose and objectives are made clear, along with timings. The background and what has driven the need for the Day are explained. The facilitator clarifies their role and gets agreement for the ground rules. It is important that an atmosphere of trust is quickly established.

A sensitive but engaging introductory exercise is in order to help team members re-establish communication which may have broken down. See icebreaker *Mad Money* in Chapter 9.

By the end of the exercise, people will be more able to express their views.

 ### SHARK ALERT! POTENTIAL PITFALL

With cynicism prevalent, people may be feeling particularly raw and vulnerable. Don't pick on individuals. Small group work will enable quieter ones to voice their opinions in a less public environment.

STEP 2: GENERATING STEAM

Objectives for Step 2
- To allow people to have their say and give vent to feelings. Bring the group back to the main point of discussion if they have become distracted by unrelated issues.
- To introduce the 'parking zone' or 'issue sheet': a flip-charted area where interesting and essential ideas that fall outside the immediate topics can be captured to be addressed at a later time.

 ### SHARK ALERT! POTENTIAL PITFALL

This is an essential step. If you try to omit or shorten it, stored up resentment will seep out throughout the rest of the event and you will find it impossible to concentrate on future action planning.

Divide the group into sub-groups (minimum of 3, maximum of 6). On a clean sheet of paper, ask them to list all their complaints and frustrations about work. Focus on the present, not what has happened in the past. Give them no more than 10 to 15 minutes for this.

Groups present back their top three complaints.

STEP 3: IDENTIFYING THE REAL ISSUES

Objectives for Step 3
- To uncover and clearly define the real issues.
- To make sure that everybody has been consulted.
- To identify the main and most pressing issues.

The facilitator flipcharts all the main issues from the previous step and asks whether there are any other issues to capture. This should result in a consolidated list.

Ensure that there is a common understanding of the definition of each issue.

Prioritise the issues. Ask people to rank them by applying coloured stickers to their top choices.

The facilitator then reviews the results and feeds back to the whole group.

STEP 4: WHAT ARE THE STEPS TO GO FORWARD?

Objectives for Step 4
- To agree what to do with the results from Step 3.
- To agree how to move on.

Only once the real issues have been uncovered, defined and prioritised can the process of rebuilding morale truly begin. Be realistic about what is achievable during the event.

Suggest a process by which the group can manage its frustrations realistically. Divide into new sub-groups and ask each sub-group to develop recommendations in action plan format for managing the most pressing problems.

Essential questions for the groups to ask themselves at this stage may be:

- What are the agreed steps that need to be taken to move the group forward? These may be fairly small steps. The important point is that they are clearly defined, agreed and adhered to.
- Who will be responsible for carrying out which part of the agreed actions?
- When will they need to complete these tasks?
- What will be the system for communicating progress to those who need to know?
- How will they ensure two-way communication?
- Who will have overall accountability for the agreed actions?

Each group presents back one of their recommendations to the whole team. This should include their reasoning behind that recommendation, including the anticipated benefits from its implementation.

STEP 5: CONFIRM TEAM AND INDIVIDUAL ATTRIBUTES

Objectives for Step 5
- To create some 'feel good' energy.
- To encourage positive thinking.
- To highlight diverse strengths in the group.

The facilitator introduces a process and individual exercise called *Building on our strengths* (see Chapter 9 for instructions). Everybody participates and the facilitator debriefs (reviews) the exercise to summarise what people discovered about themselves and each other.

STEP 6: IDENTIFY SUPPORT NEEDS

Objectives for Step 6
- To help people feel part of a team.
- To encourage mutual support.
- To identify what individuals need in order to do their jobs better and how to communicate this to the managers.

This Step requires individuals to be reflective. Our suggestion is that people find a comfortable place for half an hour to ponder the following questions:

- What do you need from your manager to help you do your job better?
- What do you need from your colleagues to help you do your job better?
- What can you offer in the way of support for your colleagues and your manager?
- What will make you feel better? Be realistic!

You can introduce this by throwing out ideas to get the group started. Ask, 'Do they need ...?'

- Knowledge
- Resources
- Skills development
- Mentoring
- Coaching
- Better communication
- Praise
- Feedback.

We strongly advise that at the end of this Step, managers and team members make arrangements to meet with one another if necessary after the event. In some cases there may be time on the Day for one-to-one meetings to take place.

STEP 7: GROUP FINALE – NETWORKING EXERCISE

Objectives for Step 7
- To end on a 'high note' with a clear vision of the next steps for the team.

- To build a positive foundation from which the team can go forward.
- To mop up any outstanding issues.

Remember to issue everyone with an evaluation form so that you can gain some immediate reaction to the event. See Part Four for more information on evaluation, and Appendices J–N for choice of evaluation forms.

A recommended team exercise for ending the Day is *Adjectives for All* (see Chapter 9 for details of how to run this exercise).

... and finally

The Morale Boosting Day provides a practical framework for helping the group to dig itself out of the hole that it may be in, acknowledge how people feel and design support mechanisms to launch them more positively into the future.

RECOMMENDED ROOM LAYOUT

For more than 12 participants, divide them into smaller groups and arrange the room into Cabaret style. See Appendix B for more information.

18 *The Planning Day*

What is a Planning Day: A definition

A Planning Day gives teams a chance to take stock and to make detailed preparations for how a concept or idea will be put into practice. It is about thinking ahead and anticipating not only what you are going to need to do, but also what resources you will need to do it. It may be part of a broader strategic plan anticipating the long term, although you still need to plan for the short term to meet each milestone. Either way, you need to ensure that your plan dovetails into the corporate vision.

In order to get what you want from the Day, remember that planning is a very rational and systematic process. You will need to utilise these attributes from within your existing team and encourage those less rational thinkers to adjust their thinking to add benefit to the Planning Day.

Another aspect to the art of planning is the essential contingency plan required when Plan A fails. We have illustrated this in Chapter 8, Troubleshooting.

When to use a Planning Day

- To help you decide on the *how*.
- When there is a requirement to forecast future resources for the team, for example training and development, IT applications, recruitment.
- When the team is unsure about the next steps.
- When you want a better plan. Others may be able to contribute valuable information that you might not have.
- When others may have a better idea of the knock-on effects of your plan.
- When others can bring essential knowledge of the critical path factors, for example when things need to happen.
- If you want to implement a complex idea.
- When you want help with strategic planning.
- When you want help with operational planning.
- When you want to gain commitment from the team.
- When you want everyone to understand what needs to happen next.
- To eliminate ambiguity.
- When you want to divide a major project amongst the team and need to define each section of work.

- When you need to demonstrate to senior management that you and the team know where you are going, or when senior managers need to demonstrate that they know what the big picture is and how to get there.
- When you need to have milestones to work towards.

SHARK ALERT! POTENTIAL PITFALLS

- Avoid being dictatorial about your ideas.
- The team may try to leave the planning process up to you, either because they don't believe that they will be listened to or because they may not have a clue what to do.
- Teams can become bogged down in detailed planning instead of taking the planning process a stage at a time.
- Be wary of rushing to adopt the first workable plan that the team comes up with. Take time to ensure that the plan has sufficient depth and detail to be a useful working document and a management information tool.

Key question: What is this really about?

It is about mapping out the next steps in whatever the process might be. The decisions about what the process *is* and whether it should be implemented will usually have been taken by the time that a Planning Day is instigated. This Day is about the *how*, not the *will we do this*? The 'what are we going to do' is covered in Chapter 16 on The Decision Making Day.

Desired outcomes: What's happened as a result of the Day?

- You are more confident that the team will achieve its aims.
- The team is more confident in your leadership.
- The direction that the team will take is clear.
- You track and monitor the team's progress towards its goal at every stage.
- Any hitches or hold-ups are identified at an early stage and quickly resolved.
- People are willing to take ownership for their part of the project.
- People are willing to help others.
- The team informs the leader if problems outside their control are threatening to derail deadlines.

How? The approach

Step 1	Welcome and introductions. Background to the Day. Reviewing objectives and setting ground rules.
Step 2	Introducing the planning topic.
Step 3	Moving from key concepts to detailed design.
Step 4	Fault proofing and contingency planning.
Step 5	Promotion and presenting.
Step 6	Next steps, monitoring progress and closing the Day.

Broad outline for the Day

STEP 1: WELCOME AND INTRODUCTIONS

Objectives for Step 1
- To set the scene for the Day.
- To describe what has driven the need for the Day.
- To state objectives and agree ground rules.

The sponsor or team leader welcomes the team and introduces the Day by explaining the purpose, background and outcomes required. It is not unusual for a team brought together to plan, to know each other quite well however you may have new team members or colleagues who are new to planning.

Get the group into pairs and ask them to plan the next big social event in their personal lives. This could be a birthday celebration, an anniversary, a wedding or other important event. They have two minutes to identify the key points that they will need to consider. Their plans must be entertaining and creative.

The pairs then swap plans with one another and review whether any key milestones have been omitted.

The sponsor, leader or facilitator leads the discussion on ground rules and gains agreement (see Chapter 4). Example ground rules for the Planning Day are:

- Stick to the issues.
- Stay focused.

STEP 2: INTRODUCING THE PLANNING TOPIC

Objectives for Step 2
- To present the topic so that it is clearly understood.
- To ensure that the relevant context for the topic has been provided.
- For the team to be clear about the purpose of the plan and why they are doing it.

The team leader presents the topic, including how it fits into the context of the team's work. Allow for questions and answers (this will give you some evidence as to the level of understanding generated by your presentation). It is not wise to move on until you are very sure that your team truly understands the purpose of this plan and why they are doing it, otherwise you may find yourself with a weak and inaccurate plan which could result in you receiving insufficient budget.

Working in trios or small groups check that everyone understands the plan by asking them to formulate the key headings that will be required from beginning to end, remembering to build in milestones so that you can check progress at every step of the way. An example could be planning a change of location, where key headings could include:

- People (who will be moving, numbers).
- Equipment/furniture (what is at the new location and what will need to be taken with us or purchased).

- Communication (type of telecommunication and networking setup).
- Continuity of workflow during the move: how do you ensure that services are managed?
- Costs.
- Facilities: is there any building work or adaptation required at the new location?

Get them to work in threes to identify the headings. Ask them to map out a rough implementation plan showing the chronological steps. Try not to go into too much detail as this session is about ensuring that the right headings are in place and that people understand the sequencing that is required for the plan to work well.

Emphasise that part of the trio's task is to collate any concerns that their group may have. These need to be included in their presentation.

SHARK ALERT! POTENTIAL PITFALLS

Not picking up individual and team concerns at this point may result in two things happening. Firstly, you may have a faulty plan if you have missed some critical factors and, secondly, if people have worries that aren't attended to their issues may fester and return to bite you twice as hard later on.

Ask the groups to present back. The facilitator looks for and points out areas of similarity and seeks agreement on the best path to pursue.

STEP 3: MOVING FROM KEY CONCEPTS TO DETAILED DESIGN

Objectives for step 3
- To add the appropriate detail to the broad brush plan so that the work can be implemented within agreed timings.
- To ensure that all individual views are aired. Consultation has to end somewhere so that you end up with a concrete plan (accurately costed). This is a final opportunity for consultation before the rough outline becomes an agreed working plan.

SHARK ALERT! POTENTIAL PITFALL

There is a danger that individuals may have a zest for ownership that means they find it difficult to concede on relatively minor details at this stage.

An effective way of handling this is to relate any points of contention to the main objective of the plan by asking 'how does this comment support or obstruct achievement of the plan?'

There are many ways of adding the desired level of detail to implementation plans. Try to make this as participative and enjoyable as possible for the team, otherwise the process can be dreary.

Examples of techniques to use at this stage are given in Chapter 9. We suggest *Papering the Plan*, this technique is collaborative although it allows for individuals to add their own contributions.

STEP 4: FAULT PROOFING AND CONTINGENCY PLANNING

Objectives for Step 4
- To stand back and review the plan to double-check that all the content is realistic given current organisational conditions and team capability.
- To identify a workable fallback position. What is the minimum that we have to achieve?
- How will we measure our success?

The facilitator asks that individuals take 10 minutes to reflect on the plan. Ask that they do this in quiet contemplation, resisting the urge to chat amongst themselves.

When there are less than ten participants, ask each individual for their measured thoughts on what might hinder effective implementation, and constructive suggestions on how to improve this plan. For more than 10 participants, ask for small-group presentations and allow 20 minutes instead of 10 to take account of preparation time.

Adjust the plan accordingly.

In the same format, ask the groups to establish the measures by which they will evaluate the success of the plan. These may be qualitative (when asked, most people say they are happy with the new layout) and quantitative (no budget overspend).

If disaster strikes, what is the minimum that needs to be achieved to make this plan happen? You need to work out some alternative ways of achieving it (often called Plan B). See Chapter 8 on Troubleshooting for examples of our fallback plans.

STEP 5: PROMOTION AND PRESENTING

Objectives for Step 5
- To establish the plan's impact on others. Bearing this in mind, how will you promote the plan? Who do you need to tell and why?
- To decide who will be involved in the process.

The reason why this step is included is to ensure that those around you support you. Otherwise your plans may founder because the people around you may not understand your purpose and so have no vested interest in collaborating with you.

The facilitator consults the group on what effect they think the plan will have on others around them (internal or external). In the example of the office move, relocating to a shared building will impact on other organisations. How will you establish a cordial working relationship with them?

Encourage the team to develop a tiered impact model, with tier 1 showing those who will be impacted upon the most by the plan, through to a final tier showing those who will barely be affected by its implementation. The group can have as many tiers as they think appropriate but, as they will need to identify the action required to promote the plan to those in each tier, remind them to stay realistic. You only have so much time and resource available!

Examples of promotional activity might include:

- A newsletter
- Meetings
- Presentations

- Informal conversations
- Questionnaires
- Intranet
- E-mails.

When you have decided on who needs to be informed and for what reason, and you have selected from the above list of promotional activity, agree an action plan. Who is going to do what? To whom? By when? For example, who will be responsible for writing, approving and distributing the newsletter?

STEP 6: NEXT STEPS, MONITORING PROGRESS AND CLOSING THE DAY

Objectives for Step 6
- To agree next steps.
- To establish a monitoring mechanism.
- To ensure that there are no issues outstanding.

Agreeing the next steps forms your action plan. This will define what action needs to be taken and identifies who will be responsible for making it happen.

The facilitator will have been gathering action points throughout the day as they have arisen. The questions are:

- Is this the right action point? Is it still required?
- Who will be responsible for it?
- When does it need to be done by?
- How will the rest of us know when it is done?
- Who will monitor the plan and report progress?

The person identified as a monitor may not necessarily have the power to coerce results on the action plan but should certainly have the team's approval to keep a watchful eye on progress and flag up any delays and barriers.

Identify a team member (hopefully a volunteer but possibly a conscript) to write up the action plan and distribute to all those who need to know.

Remember to evaluate the Day by asking participants to complete an evaluation questionnaire before they leave. See Part Four for more information on evaluation, and Appendices J–N for sample questionnaires.

Close the Day, checking that there are no outstanding issues or concerns.

RECOMMENDED ROOM LAYOUT

The key issue is that everyone is comfortable and you eliminate barriers so that people can talk with one another. Be aware of any hierarchy in the room and try to give everyone seating of equal status (no top tables, bigger chairs or separate rooms for senior people).

You will need to have enough space to tack up flipchart sheets and lining paper around the room – remember this when selecting a venue for a Planning Day. See Appendix B for choice of room layouts.

19 *The Problem Solving Day*

What is a Problem Solving Day?

A DEFINITION

There has to be an understanding of the problem or problems to be solved and an agreement of the issues at stake. This process will involve using the full resource of a group. The group for the Away Day may be your existing team or you may pull a team of people together specifically for the event so that you can use a range of different skills and perspectives.

When to use a Problem Solving Day

- When you have a problem that needs solving!
- When it is useful to have a range of approaches and mindsets to explore the problem.
- To encourage the team to buy into the options and choices for solution.
- To obtain a range of options to choose from.
- To share responsibility for solving problems and deciding what to do about them.
- To empower the team.
- To utilise effective problem-solving processes.
- To decide on the way forward.
- To enhance and practise problem-solving skills (a secondary opportunity).

Key Question: What is this really about?

In order to get truly effective solutions, you need other minds to help you. A mature team will be fully engaged and ready to take responsibility for solving their problems. Away Days like this can accelerate the process to help a team develop into maturity, although it will not happen overnight.

This Day is an opportunity to provide and use tested processes and techniques for solving problems. Sound structures are more likely to produce sound solutions. The techniques encourage applied thinking, rational thought processes and deep concentrated effort.

SHARK ALERT: POTENTIAL PITFALLS

- Teams may argue over which process to use. It is therefore essential to plan beforehand which ones you have in mind.
- If someone else is facilitating the Day, you need to have discussed the planned processes with them ahead of the event.
- Teams may be split between those who think conceptually and those who consider the details and this may result in misunderstandings between people. Ensure that the team is guided, stage-by-stage, from concept to implementation or whichever direction the technique states.
- It is difficult to anticipate how long your problem-solving session will take. What is your point of achievement? Is it full solution or a range of choices? It is important that the group gets a sense of achievement or else they will accuse you of wasting their time.
- If you, as team leader, are acting as facilitator be wary about interfering too much with the groups whilst they are working. The participants may see you as domineering and biased towards an already planned outcome. Try to show how neutral you are.
- If you have several groups presenting back, there could be a danger of this becoming unwieldy and even boring for the whole group. To keep everybody contributing, get each group to put their findings on flipchart paper on the wall and everyone can look at them over lunch or alternatively each group presents back just the key points.
- Ensure that something happens quickly after the event – action points or a solution need to be implemented otherwise participants will fast lose belief in the value and effort of time out working together.

Desired outcomes: What's happened as a result of the Day?

- Problem or problems are solved, or at least part-solved.
- For part-solved problems there may be some plans for the next stages.
- A thorough process has produced what is likely to be the best solution possible.
- You will have honed the problem-solving skills of your team.
- The team will have skills that can be easily transferred to other projects.
- Your decisions will be formed from proven processes, not haphazard guesswork.
- You will hopefully have got commitment from the team because they have been involved in the process.

How? The approach

Step 1	Welcome and introductions. Background to the Day. Reviewing of objectives and agreeing ground rules.
Step 2	Introduction to problem-solving techniques.
Step 3	Solving the problems.
Step 4	Guiding and monitoring progress.
Step 5	Decision time.
Step 6	Action planning and closing the Day.

Broad outline for the Day

STEP 1: WELCOME AND INTRODUCTIONS

Objectives for Step 1

- To ensure everyone knows why they are there and what is expected of them.
- To help the participants to get to know each other, if they don't already.
- To be clear about the facilitator's purpose and role.
- To establish ground rules.
- To understand the process for the Day.

The sponsor or team leader welcomes the team and introduces the Day by explaining the purpose, background and outcomes required. The facilitator leads the agreement of ground rules (see Chapter 4 for information on setting, agreeing and using ground rules).

The facilitator also explains their own purpose and role at the event (as a guide and supporter of the day's process).

If people don't know each other help them to break down barriers by running an icebreaker exercise (see Chapter 9 for some choices).

Remind the group that you have brought them together because of their skills, their thinking styles and their differing perspectives and state that you know they will put this to good effect to fathom out sound solutions.

STEP 2: INTRODUCTION TO PROBLEM-SOLVING TECHNIQUES

Objectives for Step 2

- To ensure that everyone broadly understands the techniques (it is important that several members of the group or each sub-group fully understand the techniques so that they can further instruct their group as they work through the problem).
- To ensure that there is back-up material available on each technique.

The facilitator explains the workings of the problem-solving techniques that will be used. Ensure that key members of each team have a good knowledge of the techniques so that they can help their team members through the process.

See Appendix E for *Brainstorming*, Appendix G for *Ranking and Rating*, and Appendix H for *Cause and Effect* techniques.

Refer the group to the handouts which are available on the techniques. Alternatively you can send out information electronically as pre-event reading.

Other techniques that you may wish to find out about are:

- Force field analysis
- Solution effect diagrams
- Pareto's principle (80/20 rule)
- Process flow charts
- Frequency distribution graphs
- Scatter graphs.

There are many books about problem-solving techniques available from good booksellers.

STEP 3: SOLVING THE PROBLEMS

Objectives for Step 3
- To mix the skills and mindsets in each group.
- To identify which problem(s) will be tackled using which technique(s).

Divide the group into mixed teams. You choose an appropriate criteria so that you can utilise a variety of skills and perspectives. The aim is to get a range of attitudes or mindsets to draw on the best challenges and ideas in the formation of a solution.

The team leader and facilitator should have identified in advance what problems to give the groups to work on. They need to have roughly anticipated and planned how the session is likely to progress. The team leader needs to be clear about what outcomes they want to achieve: one problem thoroughly worked on by a range of techniques to a detailed level, or several problems worked on using one or two key techniques to a lesser point of achievement. These pre-planned problems then need to be issued to the groups and the groups reminded about their aims and objectives.

There are further options for you to consider in running this session:

- Do you want everyone to work on the same problem, concentrated effort which will result in a range of options or do you want several of your problems worked upon at the same time benefiting from the diversity of skills and problem solving techniques available?
- What is the maximum number of people that could work effectively in a team? We recommend up to eight per team.

This Step is about getting on with it and working on actual problems. You may need to give the groups a significant amount of time and attention to achieve results from this session due to the nature of the problem-solving processes which take time.

STEP 4: GUIDING AND MONITORING PROGRESS

Objectives of Step 4
- To ensure that the groups are doing the task with confidence.
- To give guidance where required.

The facilitator will move between the groups watching and listening to check that everyone is confident with the process and the techniques. The facilitator may intervene with suggestions and corrections if they think this will help.

Remind groups where their allocated points of achievement exist for their particular problem-solving task. They need to know how much detail to go into and when to stop work.

STEP 5: DECISION TIME

Objectives of Step 5

- To be sure that each group has reached their points of achievement.
- To obtain agreement on what to do next.

The facilitator will recognise when each group has reached or is reaching a point of achievement and seek to gain their input and advice on what ought to happen next with each problem. Given the resource constraints such as time and work pressure, the group or the team leader needs to decide whether to carry on and work the problems into more detail ready for implementation or to tackle some of the other problems that are plaguing them. A decision on how to go forward depends very much on the quality and quantity of solutions that the group has created so far. At this point the team leader (or empowered group) may decide to call it a day.

Sometimes a smaller group (a sub-group) volunteers to work the solution up into more detail after the event. Another way forward may be to allocate each group the task of working up their favoured solution in their own time and asking them to present their idea back at a team meeting or at a follow-on Away Day.

STEP 6: ACTION PLANNING AND CLOSING THE DAY

Objective for Step 6
- To gain team commitment to the recommended action plan.

Always try to encourage the whole team to take responsibility for next steps as this will ensure their commitment. Whatever has been decided, draw out the action points and agree next steps and follow-up.

At the end of the session all action points must be allocated to people and given timings. Any outstanding issues must be allocated to someone to deal with.

The facilitator will list up those who volunteer to carry out specific action points, what they will do, by when and the names of others who will work with them.

Any other outstanding issues must be clarified and translated into action points. Don't forget to tell participants what happens to their work. Keep in touch.

Remember to give participants an evaluation sheet so that they can tell you what they felt about the Day. See Part Four for more information about evaluation, and Appendices J–N for sample evaluation sheets.

The team leader will close the day by summarising what has happened and, more importantly, what has been achieved.

… and finally

Many 'heads' can make light work of problem solving and some of the most creative and effective solutions have been drawn from Legendary Away Days such as this one.

RECOMMENDED ROOM LAYOUT

Opt for Boardroom style if working with just one group, or Cabaret style for more groups. See Appendix B for the choices of layout.

20 *The Teambuilding Day*

What is a Teambuilding Day? A definition

A Teambuilding Day is aimed at helping the team to recognise their own potential and rousing them to *want* to be the very best team that they can be.

The key focus for the Day is to break down any communication or interpersonal barriers that may exist between team members or working groups. People need to appreciate the impact of their own role on that of others (and vice versa) and check that they have not developed an insular approach toward their work. Encouraging them to take a holistic view of their business as well as their team is essential to the success of the Teambuilding Day.

Throughout the event, the team will work together to tackle a mixture of business- and leisure-based activities and exercises with the aim of producing a more cohesive, mutually-supportive team ready to address the challenges of business.

When to use a Teambuilding Day

- When the team is dysfunctional, or not functioning as effectively as possible.
- When the team is achieving results, but can reach even higher levels of success.
- To encourage the team to operate as a cohesive unit.
- When a team is newly formed, to clearly set out the vision and goals.
- When a team isn't responding effectively to its leadership.
- If key members of the team have recently left and the team needs to refocus.
- To allow people to network with their own team members.
- To help team members get to know something about one another as people, not just colleagues, where this would benefit team-working.
- To give the team an opportunity to let their colleagues know more about their day-to-day work.
- When there is a need to enhance working relationships.
- Where it is desirable for people to understand how their role impacts on others (and vice versa) in order to enhance working relationships.

Key question: What is this really about?

When teams are really turned on to achieving their goals, no matter how effectively each individual person is working, they must make a mutual commitment to helping one another.

Dysfunctional teams can learn to work together productively. High achieving teams can reach new levels of excellence. Whatever the needs of the team, a Teambuilding Away Day provides the time and space for people to appreciate team objectives and make the commitment to go forward together.

 ## SHARK ALERT! POTENTIAL PITFALLS

- Some people's fear of personal disclosure. Even though it may be helpful to get people to reveal something about themselves as human beings, don't be tempted to encourage team members to pry into what makes others 'tick'. Some people are less comfortable with sharing information about themselves than others. Keep teambuilding activities safe for people, inviting them to talk about areas of their own choosing, for example, their homes, families, pastimes, leisure activities.
- If the team isn't currently working well, people may be afraid of being blamed.
- When you run activities that involve people presenting, make sure to share out air time in an equitable way. Effective teambuilding demands that each team member feels valued, and permitting some to hog the limelight will be counter-productive.
- Resist the attraction of 'centre stage'. If you are team leader, consider using someone else as facilitator on the Teambuilding Day. Even though you may be team leader and the final decisions may be yours, your role in a Teambuilding Day is to be one of the team!
- As team leader, people may constantly look to you for approval or opinion on how activities should be run. Stay supportive of others and limit your input to guiding and suggesting ways forward. Don't prescribe.
- In the early stages of the Day, people may be letting existing rivalries and misconceptions affect their relationships with colleagues. Be alert to this. Don't become personally involved and do use the agreed ground rules to help people adjust their thinking toward others.

Desired outcomes: What's happened as a result of the Day?

- People enjoy working together.
- Misconceptions about one another have been dispelled or corrected.
- People have laughed *with* each other, not *at* each other!
- Team members understand the impact of their role and behaviour on their colleagues.
- People appreciate the constraints that others are working under.
- People have been able to explain their own pressures and constraints to others.
- People know one another better as individuals, not just as colleagues.
- People are ready to address workplace challenges together.
- The team demonstrates positive, mutually-supportive behaviour.
- Where potential for conflict exists, people opt to communicate and resolve it together rather than avoid it.
- Team objectives are clearly understood and people are committed to their achievement
- Group identity is strong.
- A high degree of trust exists between team members.
- Learning and development is encouraged and evaluated on a continuous basis.
- Team members coach each other.
- People are receptive to attending and contributing at team meetings.
- Team members acknowledge each others' contributions and celebrate accomplishments.

How? The approach

Step 1   Welcome and introductions. Background to the Day. Reviewing objectives and setting and agreeing ground rules.
Step 2   Warming up – breaking down inhibitions.
Step 3   Introducing and addressing the team objective(s) for the Day, for example: How can we improve team communication in the future?
Step 4   Individual and group commitment to meeting the team objective(s).
Step 5   Addressing next steps and closing the Day.

Broad outline for the Day

STEP 1: WELCOME AND INTRODUCTIONS

Objectives for Step 1
- To build people's confidence in one another and the facilitator.
- To help people understand the central role of teambuilding in meeting group targets.
- To encourage participant interest and curiosity.
- To allay fears about the need for personal disclosure.
- To agree ground rules and set standards for the running of the Day.
- To set the tone for the Day – safe and enjoyable.

The team leader welcomes participants and introduces the Day, giving brief but informative comment about the agenda, objectives and background to the Day. There may be a huge variety of drivers leading to a Teambuilding Day, each of which is holding back the team from performing at optimum capacity. The idea is to encourage people to *want* to work more effectively with their team-mates to achieve team objectives, so the introductions should be welcoming and designed to build confidence by reassuring people that they are not going to be assessed during the Day. There may be some hesitancy about what the Day will hold so the tone should be cheerful, buoyant and non-threatening. This is a moment for optimism, not for apportioning blame about what *isn't* working properly.

   The facilitator leads the agreement of ground rules (see Chapter 4). Key ground rules for the Teambuilding Day might include:

- Everyone to recognise their role as a team member.
- Support for colleagues to be maintained throughout the Day.
- Once the payback to activities is clearly explained and accepted, everyone to be prepared to participate.
- Previous judgements about others are irrelevant to the Day.
- Any personality clashes or issues to be dealt with objectively.
- All criticism to be constructive.
- Ideas to be shared freely with the whole group.
- Ideas to be heard with an open mind.
- No 'factions' to develop within the group.

Introductory exercise At this stage the group may not be relaxed and willingness to participate may be patchy. This is likely to be born more out of nervousness than dogged reluctance to join in, so ease people into the spirit of the Day with a quick, upbeat activity that sets the desired tone. See Chapter 9 for example icebreakers to choose from.

As extra security for those team members who need it, it is a good idea to run the team game as an exercise in pairs with one team member feeding back information on their partner to the whole group (see Chapter 9 for example team exercises, all of which are suitable). This will be less daunting for many people than expecting them to talk about themselves and it has the added bonus of helping them network from the start of the Day. They may already have learned something about one other member of the group that they didn't know before!

STEP 2: WARMING UP

Objectives for Step 2
- To develop trust between group members so that they become less inhibited about making personal disclosure.
- To begin to see one another as people, not only as colleagues.

Step 2 is designed to demonstrate that the Day should be enjoyable and that people will not be bullied into sharing their deepest, darkest thoughts with others. It may be useful for the facilitator to introduce Step 2 in this way! Our recommendation at this stage is to introduce an agreeable activity that is intended to raise a smile.

At Step 2, other activities should be included which are solely designed to build team togetherness. These could be anything from vox pops to drawings: the only limit is your own imagination. If people enjoy working together they will talk about these activities when they return to work and the energy and pleasure they felt on the Day will transfer itself to their working life – a truly 'can't lose' outcome!

STEP 3: INTRODUCING AND ADDRESSING THE TEAM OBJECTIVE(S) FOR THE DAY

Objectives for Step 3
- To highlight and begin to address key goals for the Day. These might include those mentioned under the heading *When to use a Teambuilding Day* above and can also include:

  - Achieving better communication within the team.
  - Developing better communication between the team and other working groups.
  - Assessing whether current working practices help or hinder communication between team members If they hinder, check whether they are still relevant. If they are not relevant then change them!

The precise activity to use at Step 3 will depend on the goals for the Day. Chapter 9 gives a selection of exercises to use in support of your Teambuilding Day. As an example, if your goal is to help the team bond more effectively, you might try *Revelation Cards*. Although this is an exercise to be completed individually, the positive feedback that participants are asked to give one another helps to forge stronger working relationships.

At this stage, the facilitator may need to deploy considerable tact and diplomacy to mediate if team members attempt to raise destructive personal issues in respect of colleagues or the group leader. Refer the group back to the ground rules. Avoid sidelining or dismissing concerns, but instead refocus the team on where it is travelling to and not where it has travelled from.

STEP 4: INDIVIDUAL AND GROUP COMMITMENT TO MEETING TEAM OBJECTIVE(S)

Objectives for Step 4
- To get team members to define and share with others their planned personal contribution to achieving the team objective.

The following two-stage exercise is designed to allow team members to show their commitment in an imaginative way.

At Stage 1, each team member makes a commitment to achieving team objectives by either:

1 Verbal presentation: planning and presenting a one minute talk, for example how they see their contribution to achievement of team objectives or how they plan to help move the team forward.
2 Visual representation: drawing a poster or picture to present back to the team on similar lines as above.

At Stage 2, the group works together to make a team commitment to achieving its goals. The form this takes will depend on how creative the group wishes to be, as well as how much time you have available for them to plan. Give the group as much time as possible for this stage and allow them licence to design their own format for the team commitment. The one proviso is that every member of the group *must* take part in the feedback. Examples might include:

- Songs
- Poems or limericks
- Mime
- Pantomime or music hall shows
- Plays
- Advertising jingles
- Building a structure made from paper or other available materials to use in the feedback.

You can also provide props for the team to use. We have seen puppet shows created to excellent effect!

STEP 5: ADDRESSING NEXT STEPS AND CLOSING THE DAY

Objectives for Step 5
Step 5 looks to gain agreement for the next part of the process, dependent on the agreed objectives for the Day (at Step 3). This also covers closing the Day. The objectives for this Step are:

- To end the event on a motivational note.
- To leave everyone feeling that they have a real role to play in the team.

If the goal was to achieve better teamworking this Step is relatively straightforward. You may ask team members to work in syndicate groups to draw up a charter for working together in the future, incorporating agreed behaviours. Ideas can be pulled together on a flipchart, with the facilitator or team leader committing to circulate the charter to all team members after the event.

More complex team objectives can be subject to the same process however you will need to allow more time for open debate and modification of ideas. Remember to apportion joint responsibility to all team members for making the action plan work. Everyone owns the plan.

Close the Day by thanking everyone for attending and for their participation. By this time of the Day, participants may have expended considerable energy and may be feeling fatigued, so keep your closing brief, to the point and as positive as you can, even if you are feeling tired yourself.

Before the participants leave remember to request completion of evaluation forms to gather views on how they viewed the Away Day. See Part Four, and Appendices J–N for evaluation templates.

Follow up

As team leader you will be able to see the 'proof of the pudding' in the coming weeks and months. Now that expectations have been set, you are in a stronger position to address issues if they occur.

... and finally

The Teambuilding Day is an investment in the team's time that will repay itself many times over. Get it right, and your team will never look back as it scales ever-greater heights!

RECOMMENDED ROOM LAYOUT

For more than 12 participants, break them into smaller groups and arrange the room into Cabaret style. See Appendix B for more information.

FOUR *After the Event*

21 *Evaluating your Away Day*

Why evaluate your Away Days? Why spend time reviewing and reflecting on your performance and the activities and outcomes involved? It may all seem like unnecessary extra work. We believe evaluation is essential because:

- It tells you if the event helped to deliver the business objectives of the organisation and the department or group.
- It tells you when something didn't go well and gives you the chance to put it right.
- You can put lessons learned into the design and running of your next event.
- People expect it: it is regarded as good practice especially if you are concerned about how the event is perceived by others.
- People like to tell you their opinions; they like to feel consulted.
- People often have excellent ideas for improving team events that you may never have thought of yourselves.
- You can uncover aspects about a team's relationship that you may have been oblivious to
- You can get a measure of how important organisational messages and themes have gone down with groups.
- You can assess how open or closed your organisational culture is by the way that people completed their questionnaires; for example in an open culture people feel confident in giving you open, frank and constructive feedback. They are usually happy to give you their names. In a closed culture you will often see marks given without any comment by anonymous people.
- You can give participating leaders any feedback, especially personal feedback from the evaluation, in such a way that it is all pooled together and kept confidential so that no one individual can be identified.
- You can give leaders necessary but sensitive feedback by collating the evaluation results so that no one individual needs to shoulder any comeback if there is any.
- It helps you to continually improve.
- It tells you if you have helped to enhance job satisfaction – perhaps a Problem Solving Away Day has improved work processes.
- It measures success against the investment of time and resources.

The four levels of evaluation – a framework

Best practice in evaluation generates feedback at four levels (Kirkpatrick model). These are:

1 Reaction – gathering participant reaction immediately after an event. Easy to obtain, this provides the participants' initial thoughts on the event and their experience. See Appendices J–N for quick or informal or visual reaction questionnaires and techniques for evaluating at this level.
2 Learning and rethinking – assessing the change in knowledge, skills or attitudes with respect to the event objectives and purpose.
3 Behaviour – showing evidence of changed ways of behaving or doing things differently as a result of the Day, for example team members communicating more effectively with each other.
4 Results – the measurable impact on the organisation; the bottom-line contribution of the event, for example increases in productivity, sales, output, quality of product or service.

Practical ways of doing it

- Develop a simple Evaluation Plan for each event. This will ensure that all Away Days have clear objectives linked to corporate and group/department needs. Know how success will be judged. Where appropriate, build evaluation activities into the design of the event, for example a session to review achievements of the day or time-out during the event to assess productivity of the process being used. Where events are interdependent or part of a sequence, get the group to evaluate progress from one event to another.
- Use post-event questionnaires to collect initial reactions (Level 1). These could be IT-based to save effort and costs (see Appendices J–N for ideas).
- A more systematic approach to evaluating behavioural change and organisational benefits is to use a variety of tools such as: face-to-face and telephone interviews; focus groups (getting a sample of participants together to facilitate discussions about what has happened differently and their reactions to the changes if any); follow-up questionnaires and surveys.
- Encourage other colleagues to evaluate their events so that there is a consistent measurement and communication of success and improvement throughout the organisation. Improving the effectiveness of Away Days will ensure that they continue to not only stimulate participants but also produce results in the most resource efficient way.

 SHARK ALERT! POTENTIAL PITFALLS

- Management or senior management often wants to know how well an event or events are being received, however they may use their own criteria for success. Why not pre-empt them by distributing your own evaluation report as quickly as possible?
- Whilst 'happy sheets' completed at the end of the Day give you some data, you have no idea of the overall impact on the organisation. For this you will need longer term evaluation through methods such as in-depth surveys, interviews with a sample of staff and focus groups.
- Not enough time? Making time in the event design for evaluation will gradually become automatic to you and will give appropriate balance on the day with opportunity for reflection as well as space for problem identification and solution finding. For a choice of

evaluation forms that you can use at the end of your Away Day, see Appendices J–N including a leader's post-event self-evaluation questionnaire (Appendix J).

The finale

Evaluation is the final part of an Away Day design and follow-up. You now have everything you need in your armoury to plan, design, run and evaluate a Legendary Away Day.

Take advantage of the supporting questionnaires in the Appendices to save you time and stimulate ideas for your own designs. We have also included a vital checklist of signs to look out for when evaluating team cohesion. The *Signposts to team success* (Appendix I) give you a benchmark against which to assess your team. This is especially useful following a Teambuilding Away Day (Chapter 20).

Remember also to review yourself using the leader's post-event questionnaire, so that you build a personal reputation for excellence.

Good luck with your Away Days. We wish you well.

Appendices

Appendix A

PRECISE PRACTICALITIES CHECKLIST

Tips to help you get started and to check your progress …

- Will an external venue be preferable, or is it more appropriate to hold this event in-house?
- What message do we want to convey with this event? What type of venue will do this most accurately?
- Is this type of venue available at a price which fits our budget?
- Are we aware of the venue's cancellation policy? What is the latest date on which we could cancel a booking without charge?
- Do we need syndicate rooms? How many? Is there a cost involved for them? If so, is it realistic for us?
- How will we resource the event? How many participants are we expecting?
- What activities will we be running? What impact will this have on the level of support needed to help facilitate the day?
- Have we identified and appointed a 'runner' for the day? Have we discussed our requirements with them so that there is no room for confusion or ambiguity?
- What room layout(s) will we need? Has this information been communicated and confirmed with the necessary parties?
- What equipment will we need? Have we confirmed that it will be available at our event? Who do we contact in the event of breakdown in equipment?
- What are our start and finish times for the event?
- Have we agreed menus and details of refreshments, including timings, with the venue? Have we checked whether there are any specific dietary requirements amongst our participants? If so, have these been communicated to the catering providers?
- Have we decided whether there will be any pre-event materials? If so, have we arranged for sufficient copies to be printed and transported to the venue?
- Have we decided on our handouts for the day? If so, the same questions apply.
- Will we need any other materials for the day? If so, have these been ordered or purchased in good time?
- Will there be any post-event documentation needed? If so, what checks have we put in place to ensure that these will be circulated as soon as possible after the event and that they are completed and returned?
- Have we settled on an appropriate style and wording for our invitations? When will invitations be sent out? Are we inviting the right people to the event? Have we addressed the 'key points' and 'inclusions' on our invitations?
- Have we sent out clear guidelines on appropriate dress code for the event?
- Have we tried to guide people's expectations about the event as accurately as possible?
- Are there any other points that we should note in respect of this event?

Appendix B

SUGGESTED ROOM LAYOUTS

 = Participants   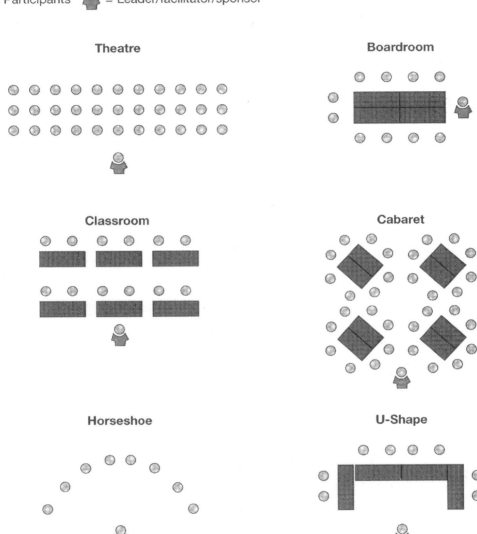 = Leader/facilitator/sponsor

Appendix C

EVENT REQUIREMENT FORM

To: ....

From: ....

Date:.. Date(s) of event: ....

Name of event:.. Number of attendees:...........................

Your details

Event leader/main contact: ....

Contact tel. no: ....

Contact email address: ....

Contact fax: ....

Address:..

Event timings: Day 1: ....

                     Day 2 (if applicable):..

                     Day 3 (if applicable):..

Timings for subsequent days (if applicable):..

Refreshment requirements   COST

Tea/coffee (please delete if not required): ....

Times required: ....

Any other refreshment requirements (biscuits, cakes, pastries): ....

....

Lunch requirements   COST

Timing: ....

Buffet/sit down lunch: ....

Any special dietary requirements (eg. vegetarian, vegan, kosher, diabetic): ....

....

Equipment requirements (delete as applicable and state quantity required)   COST

Flipchart:	yes / no	
Laptop & projector (PowerPoint):	yes / no	
TV/video recorder:	yes / no	
CCTV equipment for playback:	yes / no	
OHP & screen:	yes / no	

Other: ....

Room requirements   COST

Number of syndicate rooms required:..

Equipment required in each syndicate room: ....

TOTAL COST: ....

Appendix D

TEAMBUILDING DAY PRE-EVENT QUESTIONNAIRE

Event date:

In order to make the forthcoming Teambuilding Day the best it can be, a pre-event question-naire has been prepared to take your views into account. Your comments will help the external event facilitator design an appropriately useful and interesting day for you. All responses will be treated confidentially.

Please complete and fax/email as per the note below by _____ Thanks.

Name _____

Position _____

Division/Department/Section _____

Contact details _____

1 How is the team doing? What is going well? What isn't, if anything?

2 How well do team members communicate with each other? Does everyone know what's going on? What are the current team communication issues, if any?

3 What do you think the team needs to do to improve/ to become more successful
   (a) on the day?

   (b) in general?

4 What would make the day successful for you?

5 Any other relevant information (the state of things at present, any great ideas for the day, etc.).

6 Do you have any special needs: dietary, access, room layout, technical or any other, that we can try and provide for you.

Thank you for completing this questionnaire.
Please return to   on fax   or e-mail to

Appendix E

BRAINSTORMING (WORDBLASTING)

What is it?
Brainstorming is a technique which encourages creative thinking and the generation of ideas. It is often used as a problem-solving tool as well as being a commonly used way to draw out innovative and lateral thought.

Most groups really enjoy working together using this technique.

When to use it
- When generating a list of problems and opportunities.
- For identifying a large quantity of ideas.
- For generating possible solutions.
- For developing action plans.
- As a way of considering a wide range of angles on an issue.

What does it achieve?
Provided the rules and principles are carefully followed, brainstorming can achieve the following results:

- Many ideas are produced in a short time.
- The creation of 'unusual' ideas is encouraged.
- It encourages deeper thinking about particular issues.
- Creates a team environment.
- Provides a positive atmosphere in which to tackle problem solving.
- Enables people to contribute individually and to benefit from hearing and seeing the ideas thought up by others.

Brainstorming rules
- Avoid criticism
- Encourage any ideas – freewheel
- Quantity of ideas first
- Record all ideas
- Reflect on ideas – incubate
- Add any more ideas.

How to do it
Someone acts as the scribe, whilst everyone in the group shouts out ideas. All ideas must be written up on flipchart sheets. Make sure that everyone can see all of the ideas all of the time, so stick complete sheets to the wall. If few ideas seem to be flowing out of the minds of group members, the scribe can draw a little picture or shape or even show a prop of some sort (for example, a ball or vase of flowers) to jog minds into a slightly different gear. When all ideas have dried up, reflect on and incubate the scribed ones to push thinking even further and build on the existing ideas; even those that may have seemed silly at first. These final ideas can often be of a high quality.

SHARK ALERT! POTENTIAL PITFALLS

Not everyone calls this technique *brainstorming* as it is also terminology used in the context of epilepsy. Out of respect for this, you could choose some other term such as *wordblasting* or *ideas shower.*

Appendix F

CREATIVITY TOOLS

1 WORD ASSOCIATION – a classic creativity technique that links associated ideas. Decisions about how the ideas will be utilised, if at all, are usually deferred until later in the process.

Without any pre-conceptions about how or if the ideas could be used, create chains of association as one word or idea leads you to think of another. For example take the word 'Red'. What does it make you think of? 'Rag' (red rag to a bull) or 'flag' (keep the red flag flying)?

Let each new word lead you to think of another word. The sequence could go a bit like this:

RED – ROSE – PERFUME – SPRING – BUD – GREEN – FRESH – NEW – PERFECT
RED – FLAG – FIGHTING – BOXING – TAI CHI – GRACEFULNESS
RED – RASH – ACNE – YOUTH – STAMINA – LONG DISTANCE RUNNER – TANZANIA – HEROES
RED – SKY – SHEPHERD – MOORS – SNOW – REMOTE – SCOTLAND

Having created some lists of words, stop and look at your work. What ideas can you develop further or has it sparked some practical ideas about potential solutions or innovations for work related issues?

You can see how this tool is a boon for creative writers who can draw out descriptive groupings of words to bring their work to life or make it stand out.

2 RED RAGS – deliberately create a provocative statement. Make sure it is ridiculous or antagonistic – glean the responses, which may be incredulous or interesting. Develop the responses further to see whether any can be of use. An example might be 'cars have feelings too'. What does this make you think of? Perhaps you could capture some responses or ideas by switching around your thinking on work issues in a way that makes you think about them differently. For example – if you were your car how would you feel about the way you are treated by you and your family. Take the analogy a bit further 'if you were your team's communication process how would you feel? Ignored, never updated, old fashioned not really fit for purpose. What would make you happy? A new way of doing things, more attention, a keeper or owner, some new toys, etc.

3 BRAINSTORMING (WORDBLASTING) – a proven process for generating a large volume of ideas before evaluating them. The objective should be clearly stated and understood (for example: What can our factory do with an overcooked batch of expensive biscuits?). Nothing is discounted or judged at this stage – ideas are quickly gathered and scribed on flipchart paper until the group has no more suggestions. Following stages are prioritising and evaluating. See appendix E for more information on Brainstorming (Wordblasting).

4 MINING FOR GEMS - this is an ordered search for good ideas which involves digging your way through all ideas to sift out the jewels. This could follow on from a Brainstorming exercise or a Word Association exercise. Look at the ideas that please you and try to identify why this is the case. Do the ideas adhere to good practice? Are they practical within your team/department/organisation? Try to use original ideas – even keep a file of ideas as they occur to you or as you see them in books or magazines. They may be of use in the future. Conversations with interesting people are great sources of gems too.

5 MESSING ABOUT – children's play is a powerful way to learn through messing about with objects and ideas until a random productive outcome is achieved. The free association has full reign and the boundaries are lifted. The approach is to be enquiring, non-judgemental – and to have fun messing about! Messing about can result in a chance combination of ideas that begin to make sense as a realistic possibility to try out.

6 SPIDERGRAMS – to create a visual prompt to help you explore your ideas through to implementation. This tool works on the basis that some of us think in a non-linear way. The main issue or problem under consideration is represented in a circle in the centre of a blank page. The 'spider's legs' spin out from the centre circle and each represents a connection to the main theme. The connection is labelled at the end of the 'leg' and all issues related to that connection are noted underneath along its length. There is no limit to the number of 'spider's legs'. Connections can also be drawn from one leg to another, creating a webbed diagram. (See Figure F.1.)

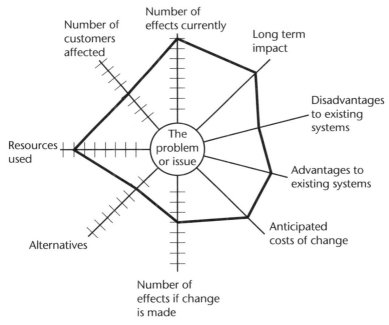

Figure F.1 Example of a Spidergram

7 COMPARISONS – moving from the concrete problem to the more abstract or general and then returning to the original problem and looking at it from the perspective of the comparisons that you made at the abstract level.

Example: you keep getting punctures in your car tyres. You move from the concrete problem with your car to the more abstract area of transport in general. List all the different types of transport. Pick one (for example, planes) and compare your problem with that of the plane – how, if your car was a plane, would you solve the problem? Planes have specialist tyres designed to be are resilient. Is anything like this available on the car tyre market?

Compare your car to the next form of transport and so on until you find some great ideas to test out.

INSPIRATION – taking inspiration from the world around us that sparks ideas for a design or process. Leonardo da Vinci examined common insects and winged creatures to gain inspiration for his helicopter designs. Other people's processes are well worth exploring to see if they can improve the processes currently used in your organisation, for example Systems Thinking (a method of explaining how people and processes link together and relate to each other) is used to help families solve their difficulties in a therapeutic context, but it can also be used to gain better understanding of how groups and organisations have become blocked and can solve their relationship and process problems.

OPPOSITES – dare to think the opposite of what is expected. The important thing is to create surprise (for example, advertising traditional Christmas drinks during the summer). This is a great exercise to use when trying to think of new sales ideas for test marketing. The question for the group may be 'How could we expand/increase sales of our product which has historically only sold to a certain segment at a certain time of the year?' Thinking the opposite of the expected and imagining millions of people eating Christmas pudding on a desert island in the full glare of the sun might lead you to think of Christmas-pudding-flavoured ice cream which could, in turn, lead you to think of all the different winter flavours and summer flavours that you could create to expand your ice cream business.

The approach to aim for when using any of these Creativity Tools is:

- BE CREATIVE

- BE NON-JUDGEMENTAL

- BE POSITIVE

- BE OPEN.

Appendix G

RANKING AND RATING

What is it?
Ranking is a structured process of placing a number of options in order of preference, by using a scoring system which is called rating.

Why use it?
- Helps to choose the best options
- Makes the choice less emotional
- Increases the ownership of the chosen option.

When to use it?
- For deciding on which problem to tackle
- For deciding on which solution to implement
- For deciding on which alternative to choose.

How to use it?
1 List the options
2 List the selection criteria
3 Categorise the criteria (essential/desirable)
4 Test the options against essential criteria
5 Rate the remaining options.

Example – Selecting an event facilitator
1 List the options – facilitators A–K
2 List the criteria
3 Categorise the criteria
4 Test against essential criteria
   (two examples shown)

	Weighting*	
*10 is high	Essential	Desirable (weighting)
Appropriate skills	✔	
Appropriate experience		2
Personal style		10
Accurate brief		5
Enthusiasm		10
Price		5
Availability	✔	

Facilitator	Availability	Skills	Overall
A	✔	✔	✔
B	✗	✗	✗
C	✔	✔	✔
D	✔	✗	✗
E	✔	✔	✔
F	✔	✔	✔
G	✔	✔	✔
H	✔	✔	✔
J	✔	✔	✔
K	✔	✔	✔

5 Rate the remaining options against the desirable criteria

Criteria	Experience	Style	Brief	Enthusiasm	Price	Total
Weighting	2	10	5	10	5	Max=32
Facilitator						
A	1	3	4	7	2	17
C	2	6	1	5	4	18
E	0	4	1	2	1	8
G	1	6	3	4	4	18
H	2	7	4	6	5	24
J	1	5	4	8	2	20
K	1	8	5	4	1	19

Facilitator H is the preferred option.

Appendix H

CAUSE AND EFFECT ANALYSIS

What is it?
Cause and Effect Analysis is a technique for identifying the possible causes of a problem. A Cause and Effect diagram is a simple yet clear method of visually recording possible causes relating to the effects.

Why use it?
- Helps break down large problems into smaller chunks.
- Helps generate ideas.
- Provides a method for recording ideas.
- Reveals hidden relationships between causes and effects.
- Helps identify the root of a problem.

When to use it?
- For defining a problem
- For identifying possible causes
- For developing objectives for solutions
- For narrowing down causes
- For solving problems.

How to construct a Cause and Effect diagram (fishbone style)

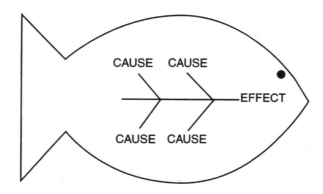

- Name the problem in terms of its effect.
- Identify the major categories of causes, for example: machines, methods, materials, manpower or technology, processes, resources and people.
- Sometimes it is worthwhile to stop and allow ideas time to incubate.
- Analyse the possible causes and indentify any 'linkages' between the possible causes (if any).
- Evaluate the most likely causes (or combinations) and agree to focus on these for corrective action.

Ground rules for success

- Involve everyone.
- Use large diagrams.
- Examine causal relationships.
- If too many causes established, redefine effect.
- When brainstorming possible causes, try not to be judgemental or evaluate ideas too early.
- Identify the possible causes.

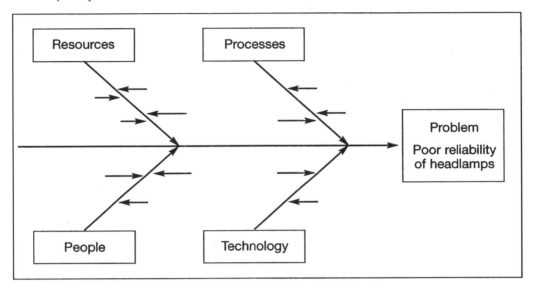

Use Brainstorming for each of the main categories.

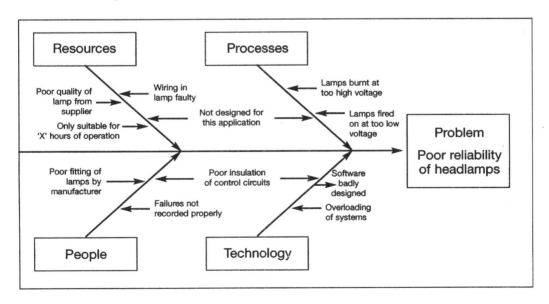

Appendix I

SIGNPOSTS TO TEAM SUCCESS

- Purpose   Clear/committed.
- Vision   Powerful/inspirational.
- Values   Implied in the purpose and vision, refer to when making tough decisions.
- Clarity   Roles and commitments.
- Project   Group invents projects to achieve its purpose.
- Identity   Strong. Trust developed through honesty with each other.
- Communication   Agree ways to work through conflict rather than avoid it. Group communicates even when it's hard.
- Learning   Monitoring and evaluating as go along.
- Acknowledgement Of each other's contributions.
- Celebration   Group celebrates accomplishments.

Appendix J

POST-EVENT LEADER SELF-EVALUATION

Completing a concise leader self-evaluation form after a team event fulfils several purposes:

- It enables you to assess how successful the event has been. Did the team meet its objectives?
- It clearly highlights your personal contribution to the event – what worked well and what could be done differently next time.
- It gives guidance for improving your performance at future events.
- It points out your strengths in facilitation and also areas for development.

The following questions will focus your thinking and enable you to form a realistic view of what the event has accomplished – and your part in it.

Questions to ask yourself

1 To what extent did the group achieve its objectives? How do I know?
2 To what extent were individual participants satisfied with the event? How do I know?
3 Were there any unexpected positive or negative outcomes from the event? What did I do about the negative outcomes, if any?
4 Was I realistic about setting the objectives for the event? How do I know?
5 Did I clearly communicate the objectives for the event? How do I know they were understood?
6 Am I satisfied with the event programme? Did the design help us meet our objectives? If so, how?
7 Did I ensure that suppliers, contractors, facilitators and specialists were accurately briefed?
8 Did the setting and agreeing of ground rules support the team's progress?
9 Am I happy with the way in which I worked with participants during the event?
10 How effectively did I fulfil my event role?

Appendix K

EVALUATION QUESTIONNAIRE (DETAILED)

Away Day title   Date   Venue

It would be hugely helpful if you could give me, the facilitator, some feedback about today. If you wish to remain anonymous just leave your name off this form.

Your Name and Department _____

_____

1 Did you gain any benefit from today? If so, how?

2 Was there anything that you thought was excellent or very good about the day? If so, what?

3 Was there anything that you thought was negative about the day? If so, what?

4 What, if anything, do you think should happen now as a result of the day?

5 What are you personally going to do as a result of today? Any actions?

6 What did you think about the speakers at the event? Constructive comments about them are welcome.

7 What did you think about the facilitation of the day? What was helpful or unhelpful regarding the process of the event?

8 What did you think about the venue, including the food? All your comments will help us choose suitable venues for you in the future.

9 Do you have any other comments that could help us improve the design and running of events for you?

Thank you very much for your time and thoughts – please give this form to:

_____

Appendix L

GROUP EVALUATION (QUICK ZOOM AROUND)

For a fast and easy-to-accomplish assessment about what participants may have gained from an Away Day. This brief form works well with groups of less than 15 members. Ask each participant to make a statement concerning the one most significant gain from the event for him or her. This procedure generates considerable data about the immediate reaction to the event.

You can extend the zoom around by asking one or two additional questions. Choose from the following or think up some of your own.

- The most significant thing to me during this event was...
- What I intend to apply or do differently as a result of this event is..
- What I want to happen now is ....
- What I intend to do now is ....
- What still needs to be done or addressed is ....
- My wishes for this group are..
- I understand..better than I did before
- The best moment of the event was..
- The funniest thing about the event was ....
- The most difficult thing about the event was...

Appendix M

FACES EVALUATION QUESTIONNAIRE

Event title:

Date:

Please take the time to complete this short evaluation form. Although positive feedback is always welcome, negative comments help us to meet your future needs.

Name (optional)_____

Please tick under the cartoon which most nearly depicts your feelings

	☺	😐	☹
Pre-event administration and information			
Keynote speaker (name):			
Guest speaker (name):			
Venue			
Refreshments			
Opportunity to network			
Facilitators			
Event outcomes reached			

Comments:..
....
....

Please complete this before you leave today and hand it to the facilitator. Thank you.

Appendix N

EVENT EVALUATION QUESTIONNAIRE

Please rate the following points by ticking the appropriate box
(if 'poor' please comment at the end of the form)

1 Overall rating of the day

Excellent	Good	Fair	Poor
❑	❑	❑	❑

2 Day's objectives *(please indicate the extent to which you feel the day's objectives were met)*

Excellent	Good	Fair	Poor
❑	❑	❑	❑

3 Programme content *(and its relevance to the overall objectives)*

Excellent	Good	Fair	Poor
❑	❑	❑	❑

Activities

Excellent	Good	Fair	Poor
❑	❑	❑	❑

Speakers

Excellent	Good	Fair	Poor
❑	❑	❑	❑

Amount of discussion

Excellent	Good	Fair	Poor
❑	❑	❑	❑

4 Facilitator/leader/sponsor

Excellent	Good	Fair	Poor
❑	❑	❑	❑

Group involvement

Excellent	Good	Fair	Poor
❑	❑	❑	❑

5 Handouts

Excellent	Good	Fair	Poor
❑	❑	❑	❑

6 Visual aids

Excellent	Good	Fair	Poor
❑	❑	❑	❑

7 Venue/refreshments

Excellent	Good	Fair	Poor
❑	❑	❑	❑

8 Pre-event administration/information

Excellent	Good	Fair	Poor
❑	❑	❑	❑

continued overleaf…

9 What were the positives of the event?

10 What are your suggestions for improvement?

11 Any other comments?

Thank you for attending this event and for taking the time to complete this evaluation.

Contacting the authors

Contacting the authors

If you wish to have further support at any of your Away Days, both authors are available as facilitators and can be contacted as follows:

Karen Cooley
01233 500289
07790 037626

karenc@cglen1.fsnet.co.uk ·

Kirsty McEwan
01833 590531
07866 266644

kirsty.mcewan3@virgin.net
www.facilitator-uk.co.uk
www.kirstymcewan.co.uk

Index

Games for Legendary Away Days

Karen Cooley and Kirsty McEwan

Games for Legendary Away Days provides a range of games that have been developed and designed by the authors for use on Away Days. The 33 games are divided into 11 sections, matching the types of Away Day that the authors defined in their first book; there are games for teambuilding events, morale-boosting events, change management events, problem-solving events and so on. Selecting games that are specific to particular styles of Away Days means that the user has (virtually) a guaranteed success rate. There are content-rich games, supported by icebreakers and energizers.

Each of the games has been chosen and the text written specifically with the particular application of the given Day in mind. This means that the games are both highly appropriate to the kind of event you are running and a safe bet for injecting learning with fun.

COMING SOON IN AUTUMN 2004

GOWER

Presentation Planning and Media Relations for the Pharmaceutical Industry
John Lidstone
0 566 08536 4

Using the PC to Boost Executive Performance
Monica Seeley
0 566 08110 5

The 'How To' Guide for Managers
John Payne and Shirley Payne
0 566 07726 4

**Managerial Consulting Skills
A Practical Guide 2ed**
Charles J. Margerison
0 566 08292 6

**Creating a Thinking Organization
Groundrules for Success**
Rikki Hunt with Tony Buzan
0 566 08230 6

Guide to Internal Communication Methods
Eileen Scholes on behalf of ITEM
0 566 08217 9

Gower Handbook of Management Skills 3ed
Ed by Dorothy M. Stewart
0 566 07889 9

Proven Management Models
Sue Harding and Trevor Long
0 566 07674 8

GOWER

Contract Negotiation Handbook 3ed
P.D.V. Mars h
0 566 08021 4

The Bid Manager's Handbook
David Nickson
0 566 08512 7

Gower Handbook of Project Management 3ed
edited by J. Rodney Turner and Stephen J. Simister
0 566 08138 5 (hbk) 0 566 08397 3 (CD-ROM)

The Relationship Manager
The Next Generation of Project Management
Tony Davis and Richard Pharro
0 566 08463 5

Project Management 8ed
Dennis Lock
0 566 08578 X (hbk) 0 566 08551 8 (pbk)

Project Management for Successful Product Innovation
Alan Webb
0 566 08262 4

Managing Projects at Work
Gordon Webster
0 566 07982 8

The Essentials of Project Management 2ed
Dennis Lock
0 566 08224 1

For further information on these and all our titles visit
our website – **www.gowerpub.com**
All online orders receive a discount

GOWER

Join our email newsletter

Gower is widely recognized as one of the world's leading publishers on management and business practice. Its programmes range from 1000-page handbooks through practical manuals to popular paperbacks. These cover all the main functions of management: human resource development, sales and marketing, project management, finance, etc. Gower also produces training videos and activities manuals on a wide range of management skills.

As our list is constantly developing you may find it difficult to keep abreast of new titles. With this in mind we offer a free email news service, approximately once every two months, which provides a brief overview of the most recent titles and links into our catalogue, should you wish to read more or see sample pages.

To sign up to this service, send your request via email to **info@gowerpub.com**. Please put your email address in the body of the email as confirmation of your agreement to receive information in this way.

GOWER